SOAR

Transformational Stories of Strategy, Soul and Sensational Results in Business

Insights and Strategies From Everyday Successful Business Owners

Published by Prominence Publishing
www. Prominencepublishing.com

ISBN: 978-1-988925-69-1

Contents

Introduction

By Laurie Hawkins

As I sit down to write, I have this deep desire to share wisdom with you. It strikes me that the first thing I always do is go to my bookshelves. My way of processing anything is to find the best books on the topic, dive deep into them, and then walk away with a golden nugget of knowledge that I carry forward with me. Over time, those nuggets have been blended with experience to form the foundation of who I am. What shocks me with this thought is the books. I want to write a book, and yet the first thing I do to research a topic is go to my bookshelves. I can't go to my bookshelves to write this book...or can I? I started pulling books out - the books that have stayed on my shelf since that first pivotal book that changed my life forever, The Power of Intention by Dr. Wayne Dyer. I keep going and realize it's like the themes of my life are coming off the shelves...Braving the Wilderness, Year of Yes, Present over Perfect, Boundaries, Awakening Corporate Soul...I pull out 25 books that have shaped my life and business.

My first instinct was to share what I have learned from the most impactful books I have read. Then I realized - you can read those books yourself. It is the stories that connect with our hearts. It is the people we meet, the businesses we connect to, the experiences we live, the lives we unfold, the love we build that matters. I've always been attracted to people's stories; to how they lived through tragedy to reach triumph, how they fell and got back up, how they started from nothing to create real influence and impact in the world. We hear the stories every day and the first ones that always come to mind in this era are Apple, Microsoft, UBER, Facebook, Southwest Air, Starbucks...you get the idea. I love these stories and yet, they are so big...so BIG. Although we can take lessons away from them, in my years as a consultant I have had the amazing pleasure of working with incredible, everyday business owners whose stories compel me to my core. Their stories give me vision and insight into what is truly possible.

This book is a compilation of everyday, authentic, powerful, remarkable people and the businesses they have created. Now, if you asked each of them if they felt they were powerful and remarkable, they may stumble on the answer. They are humble, take action, connect to the heart, work deeply, focus profoundly, and make-it-happen people. Their stories are dynamic, encouraging, uplifting, empowering and, above all, make us realize that anything is possible for anyone.

As this book was in its birthing process, a worldwide crisis hit. This crisis began as a health crisis and quickly became a crisis of humanity and touched every aspect of our lives. At its core, it was asking the world to pause, to reflect, to reset, to reconsider. From a business perspective, we have yet to understand the impact and yet, what we know for sure is that every person and every business will emerge from this...different. As the days unfolded, some businesses were shut down and forced to lay off their people, while other businesses started to thrive to support the current needs of society. This uncertainty has made one thing certain – you never know what will happen to shift your business. As we continue to move through this challenge, organizations are having to reinvent themselves on the fly.

We asked each of the business owners in this book to reflect upon this and share the greatest lessons they have learned along the way that would support people in times of uncertainty. Each co-author added an addendum to their chapter called **"Then a Pandemic Hits"** to share their lessons learned. May they serve you as you emerge from these times of uncertainty. We will always remember 2020!

I am deeply grateful for the opportunity to work with every single person in this book. What I love most about the work that I do is that every person that I touch makes me a better person. They help me think differently, feel more deeply, and become the person that I am intended to be. Although I am brought into my customer's businesses (some featured in the stories shared here) to help them grow, I am the one who has the profound experience of growing alongside them. May these stories do the same for you.

CHAPTER ONE

All the Doors That Could Be Opened

By Terry Fletcher

I was somewhat humbled to be asked to write a chapter in this book about entrepreneurs. It is the story of my building a very successful company over the last 42 years. That journey began with the life lessons I learned starting at a very early age, and all the experiences that followed are what molded me into what I am today.

I was born in 1941 during World War II in Liverpool, England. It was a time of real trouble; Liverpool was getting bombed heavily. Houses all around us were destroyed and disappearing, and there were shortages of everything, particularly food. My parents lived in an air raid shelter in the backyard, taking cover from the airplanes dropping bombs all around. In many respects, I'm lucky to be alive.

When the war ended in '45, I was four years old. Because of the scarcity of everything, my parents had to be very frugal, and because of that they taught me extremely good work ethics and the value of money; if you're going to buy something, you save up, you work; do your chores, you get your spending money, and then you can go buy what it is that you want. I learned those values. I delivered green groceries on bicycles, I had paper rounds, and I worked and saved my earnings. I understood those principles of being truly sensible and responsible financially.

As a young man, I attended Manchester University, the School of Science and Technology, and there I studied for a mechanical engineering and aeronautical engineering degree. I was in a five-year apprenticeship program with an aircraft company, A.V. Roe. They paid for all the schooling, but in the summers, apprentices were required to go and work in the aircraft factory. We had the benefit of the education and the hands-on experience in the factory. At the end of it, there was a guaranteed job. I failed my first year at University because it was so hard, but I managed to finish my apprenticeship with a lower level of qualification, with a Certificate in Mechanical Engineering. The thing was, I just didn't like the work. I had a drawing board at the window, looking out of the factory where I worked. The aircraft and the guided missile work that we were designing in the factory was top secret. There was strict security to get in and out of the building, so it felt very much like being in a prison. I wanted to be on the outside, so I made the move. I left and became a sales engineering representative with different companies.

The last one I worked at I was fired from, which was a total blessing in disguise because it put me on the road to where I am today. At that time, I was unemployed for a couple of months. One of my neighbors, who knew about my predicament, was walking into the village of Macclesfield, in England, where my wife and I lived at that time. I gave the neighbor a ride into town, and she told me that her company was interviewing for salesmen just then, and asked if I'd be interested in putting my name down for a job. I said yes, though I had no idea what her position was or what the company did. I went for the interview and got the job.

The employer told me that it was straight commission. I had never been on straight commission before and didn't think that I could take it. He asked how much I was making at my last job, and I told him sixty pounds a week. He told me to take the job and he'd guarantee me sixty pounds for twelve months. I accepted the position and was trained how to sell Wynn's Oil automotive products to garages, service stations, and dealerships. I absolutely fell in love with the work and was quite successful. I stayed with them for two years and had never made as much money in my life. I was making 100 pounds or more every week, which was good money at that time.

After a couple of years, the Wynn's company changed in England, and everyone was taken off straight commission and put on salary. The top twelve salesmen were promoted to area managers in England. I was one of them; put on salary, given a company car, and an expense account. The thing was, my salary was half of what I had been making. I tried it, and it just wasn't working. I was offered a job in Canada, selling Wynn's just as it used to be in the old days, and I accepted it.

In 1975 my family and I emigrated to Canada with no money and started work near Niagara Falls, where we rented a house. It wasn't the only thing we rented; because of an unexpected financial glitch only one week before our move, we were unable to transfer our money or our possessions and ended up renting everything from silverware to furniture as well. It was at least three months before we were back on our feet again.

After a few months, the owner of the business promoted me to sales manager, to look after all his salesmen, and start selling Wynn's warranty programs to new car dealers. I had become familiar with the Wynn's warranty programs in England because Wynn's had a warranty division there. I was fascinated by the fact that they could put warranties on used cars. All new cars came with a warranty, and used cars didn't, but Wynn's had a program where a used car dealer could put a warranty on a previously owned vehicle. When I emigrated to Canada, I had the opportunity to sell Wynn's warranties, but only to new car dealers.

After two years in that position, I grew uneasy with my boss, and I started looking for another job. That's when I came up with an idea. I loved the concept of the Wynn's warranty, so I began to think that I should just do my own. I had no money though; at that point, my account balance was $300. I went to the bank and told my story to the bank manager. He said he liked me, and he liked my story. He loaned me $3000 as seed money so I could start a business. That was when Lubrico Warranty Incorporated was born.

That was enough to get me going. I could buy point of sale material and the other things I needed. I went out and started selling a twelve-month used car warranty on my own in Southwestern Ontario. Forty years ago, new cars only came with a one year warranty. It was a challenging sell; I didn't approach new car dealers at that time, because Wynn's was there, and that was a conflict of interest. Instead, I went to used car dealers who had no warranty programs. It was unique to them. The dealers were actually afraid of it because they worried that their phone would never stop ringing with claims for the cars they sold if they went out with a one year warranty.

I had to put their minds at rest that it wouldn't be their phone, it would be my phone that would ring; the warranty would be with me, not with them. Fortunately, a few dealers saw the benefit and the value of having a twelve-month warranty on a used car, which was the same as a new car. I was thankful for the dealers who initially shared my vision of what the product would mean to them.

I set up an office in my basement and worked out of it for six years, but my office address was at Maclean-Hunter Communications in London on Queens Ave, and I used that as my office address. It was more prestigious. The paging company had all kinds of toll-free 1-800 numbers, which dealers and consumers would call, thinking they were calling direct to my office, but they were calling to a paging company. The paging company would contact me while I was out in the field selling to other dealers. My pager would go off, and I would have to find a payphone that was working and call the paging company, find out what the message was and who wanted to see me, then I'd call that person and find out what they needed; whether it was a car broken down, or a dealer wanting to sign up. If it was a warranty claim, I'd send them to a repair garage to get the car checked over and make sure it was a genuine claim. Sometimes my pager would go off again while I was in there, and occasionally angry people outside the payphone box would be knocking on the side of it, asking me how much longer I was going to be. I'd apologize and finish my business as quickly as possible. The phone box was, in essence, my office. If it was today, I could have done it from the comfort of my car with a cell phone. It was one of the difficulties of running a business with no employees other than myself, but it worked. Eventually, I hired a couple of salespeople, and after six years, I did open a public office.

The warranty I sold was for engines, transmissions, and differentials, which are the major components of a used car, and the most expensive parts to fix. I wasn't selling for another company; it was my own product, and I was self-insuring. If there was a claim, I paid it. I was the risk-taker; I wasn't passing it off to anyone else. I designed it, maintained it, and serviced it. Wherever I traveled, I partnered with repair garages that I could trust the work to. I made arrangements with them ahead of time and worked out a discount on parts and labor in return for me sending them business. I was negotiating and selling all day, every day, on the road, with a pager strapped to my belt.

In 1981 I hired two salespeople to cover different parts of Ontario; one was Ottawa, and the other was Kingston. It was geographically too far for me to go, so I extended my area in Ontario with additional sales representation.

My business began to grow; it doubled in revenue every year for twelve years. It was a new concept, and dealers eventually started to get the idea. They could use the product to help sell the car, and it made them a bit more profit in their sale. Mine was the first company in the whole of Ontario to offer such a thing to used car dealers, which is why they were afraid of it. It was a unique product. It's not like a company selling widgets. You sell a widget today, and tomorrow you've got to sell more widgets. Mine was an ongoing relationship type of business. We'd build a relationship with the dealer who was selling the warranties and also build a relationship with the repair garage network, which eventually spanned the whole country. It was creating a whole network like that across the country, which helped spread the word about Lubrico.

When I first determined how much to sell the warranties for, I knew Wynn's was charging $100 for a one year warranty, so I used that, and it really worked. After a few years of experience, I got the statistics that confirmed the pricing was accurate. Math was one of my best subjects in school, so I did all of my own calculations with my expenses, my overhead, figuring out how much I needed to satisfy all future claims. I invested that reserve money (now called a trust fund) with a financial company in low-risk investments. Over time each year, I added more and more warranties and created a huge database of experience on the computers, so we could work out exactly what the trust fund needed as the business expanded. Every consumer and every dealer were protected by this cushion of excess cash in the trust fund. There was no risk. Morally, it was the right thing to do.

In my first two to three years offering warranties, I had another job at the same time, selling automotive books to the same people I was promoting warranties to; garages, mechanics, and service departments. The books were repair manuals and flat rate labor guides, which are resources that tell mechanics how to fix any make of vehicle, and how many hours it should take to do a particular job on a car, so they know how much to charge a consumer on the bill. For the mechanics and the service stations, those were their bibles. That job was also straight commission, but it kept food on my table and a roof over my head without having to touch any of the money that was coming in from Lubrico, while the trust fund was being built.

One of the first major challenges that I faced, four or five years into my endeavor, was receiving a cease and desist letter from the Superintendent of Insurance for Ontario, saying that I had no right to be in the business. It was a shock to me. They had discovered that I was selling warranties to car dealers with an insurance type of product that wasn't regulated. My products weren't regulated because I was self-insured, and the superintendent had a problem with that. They told me to close up. They sent notifications to every car dealer in Ontario stating, 'We've discovered that this company and possibly other companies are selling uninsured warranties, and if we discover you, the dealer, selling uninsured warranties, we will fine you, as you'll be in breach of insurance regulations.' When my customers received the letters, it scared them. They called me, and I heard a mix of 'I'm sorry, it's the law, I can't deal with you anymore,' and 'Are you going to continue to look after me like you've done before?' I said I'd absolutely look after them, they said they'd support me and my business, and they did. I had a core base of dealers who continued to sell. If they hadn't, my business would have folded at that time.

There was no regulation in writing then that described used car warranties, and no data available for the government to know what the fees should be. I went with my lawyer and met with them face to face, and came to an agreement. If I put $50,000 up in a trust with my lawyer, they'd allow me to continue, but I was to start looking for an insurance company that would insure me. I walked up and down all the streets in Toronto with my briefcase in hand and knocked on every door of every insurance company I could find. I explained my situation, but they looked at my business and couldn't offer me reinsurance because there was nothing in their rulebooks about my type of business. Once again, unregulated. I had to tell the Superintendent of Insurance to either find an insurance company that would underwrite the risk or get off my back. Eventually, they got off my back. I did get insurance, seven years into my business, and it gave me much more credibility over the other warranty companies that started to pop up.

Another hurdle came around many years later to bite me again. I was audited for premium tax. It was once more to do with insurance. They said I was selling insurance and not paying any taxes, so I owed them almost half a million dollars in arrear premium taxes. They went back several years on it. I was able to stay in business because I paid them the arrears of tax, but I didn't send them any more money after that because I took them to court and sued them for creating undue hardship. Due to them dragging their feet and ignoring our requests for any form of communication, it took 12 years to eventually get a trial date. It was then that they agreed to concede and paid me back in full plus interest. They were wrong in the first place to do what they did, and I could not let them get away with it. They had no case and ultimately admitted that automotive warranty companies are not regulated by the Superintendent of Insurance. No apology of course.

One of the personal challenges I faced, not only in the business but throughout a good deal of my life, has been depression. Since I was about thirty years old, I've been living on anti-depressants. It hasn't been easy, but I've gotten through it, and I know I had God's hand in it. Mine is a spiritual family, and we believe that it's been nothing short of a miracle.

I overcame all the obstacles that arose because I had a vision for this business; I knew that it was going to take off. I saw the need and I was passionate about it, which showed when I did a presentation to a dealer. It's a product that would make a dealer nothing but money without any heartache or headache at all, and it was simple. You could add it to the price of the car, or you could add a 3-month or a 6-month warranty and upsell that customer to a 2 or 3-year warranty, and start making money with it. As well as helping to sell the car, it also enabled dealers to make more profit on the sale. The warranty was designed to uplift the image of the Used Car Industry and give consumers 'peace of mind'.

I worked hard, and Lubrico experienced exponential growth for many years, mostly because of the reputation of the company. We said what we would do, and then we did what we said. A lot of companies and salesmen promise the earth, but they don't deliver. As my business developed through the years and I hired more salespeople, there was more word on the street, and I was able to pick up new dealers here, there, and everywhere. The company also expanded because of the creativity of the product and the processing of the claims. We handled claims well, and we earned the best reputation in the country for being the company to deal with. If a customer wanted value for their money, they chose us.

All my hard work paid off, and my company ended up being the best and the biggest in Canada in its niche. That's why I was finally bought out by an insurance company in 2020; one that had been a competitor of mine for many years. It began with so little, but I did a calculation a couple of years ago, and I can say that at that time, we did more business in an hour than I did my whole first year of operation. That's how much the company grew, and it is a measure of the company's success.

There are lessons learned in giving 42 years of one's life to a career commitment like I have. Before I went into business for myself, I saw things that I didn't like. Working takes up so much of your life. You spend more time at work than you do with your family most of the time. So, if you don't enjoy it, then you'd better get out of it and find something that you do enjoy. I wanted my people to feel exactly the same way; particularly the salespeople. The company created great lifestyles for my people; they made more money than they would working anywhere else, and it was a fun job.

One of the big lessons I learned was about human nature; if you treat people right, they'll treat you right. It happened on occasion that the car dealer would sell a car and sometimes the car had a problem with it, but the problem wasn't covered by the warranty. The customer felt cheated. I would settle that by saying to the dealer, 'Look, it's not your fault, it's not my fault, and it's not the consumer's fault that the car has broken down, so why don't we split the bill three ways, and just get on with life. Everyone pays a little bit, it doesn't change anyone's lifestyle, and everyone moves on; everyone's happy. We'd meet in the middle and take care of it. I tried to keep everyone satisfied, rather than a cold 'no it's not covered' answer.

Looking back, I think a lot of people wouldn't have taken the rejection I had to take, and it was frequent. In the early years, I was trying to persuade dealers that the product was good for them, but so many of them said no. A lot of them wanted me to get other dealerships around them to sign up first, and then come back to them afterward, being a follower, not a leader. It was a typical response. I got rejected all the time. Not everyone can take rejection, but I did a silly little thing when I got a no: I'd get back in my car and whistle, and I'd get out of the car and whistle all the way into the next dealer, and then I'd present again. Somehow through the whistling, I was able to drown out the rejection and just keep moving forward. The thing to remember is that it's not personal, so you can't take it personally. I had an objective; there were thousands of car dealers out there. That one might not want it, but look how many other doors are out there that could be opened. It was perseverance and patience. It might take a couple of years to get a dealer to believe, but we kept calling on him. I'd say 'don't burn your bridges.' I taught that to all my salespeople. If a dealer leaves you and goes to another company, don't burn your bridge, because it'll only be a matter of time before that warranty company breaks their heart when they don't pay for a claim that they should pay for, so you keep calling on him, and take him some coffee, take him some donuts, and keep a relationship going. Make them like you so that it would hurt their feelings to have to tell you 'No, I'm not selling you anymore.' Now there's a relationship-built business. I loved that side of my business; motivating and training my salespeople and changing their attitudes. Just treat people right; everybody, all your employees. That was so important. If they are doing a good job for you, let them know and praise them, but if they're not, you let them know that, too. Give them a chance and facilitate change.

Since Lubrico began, the company has always been about the people who are part of the team, and the team is every person who works for the corporation. It is all of them together that make this company the success that it is. It has been a true joy to treat my employees right, and to reward them for all of the hard work and dedication that they are so committed to.

We had financial incentive programs for all our internal staff, who are our unsung heroes doing all the work behind the scenes in full support of the salesforce, dealers, warranty holders and repair centres. We also had incentive programs based on volume for all our dealers, in which they earned travel rewards. Several times we took them all to Mexico, Las Vegas, and other travel venues. For the last trip to Cancun, Mexico, we had approximately 300 people at the resort. It is important to look after those who look after you.

These incentives and rewards, amongst other things, buy loyalty and help the company to stand out from the rest. It's really giving back to those who make the business what it is, and showing appreciation where it is deserved. It also gives everyone goals and a sense of achievement.

We created a culture, and it's a culture that has thrived at every level of this business; one big family, all taking care of one another. Building this company to its pinnacle has been one of the greatest accomplishments of my life.

Then a Pandemic Hits

My personal advice, particularly to young entrepreneurs:

First, I would say do not be discouraged by rejection. Stay very positive and passionate about your product or service.

Secondly, do not let your business consume you 100% to the point where you neglect your family and friends.

Finally, always save for a rainy day. Personally, I worked a second job while I was building Lubrico and I saved or reinvested every penny that I made for two years. Having savings in the bank can give you security and help you weather the storms during difficult times. If possible, do not take on huge debt; start small and build from a solid base.

.

About the Author

Terence David Fletcher was born February 4, 1941 in Liverpool, UK, during World War II to a working/middle class family with a Mum, Dad and elder sister. He began schooling at age 4 ½ years old and graduated from Northway Primary School, Liverpool at age 11 years. He then attended Quarry Bank High School in Liverpool from age 11 - 16 years and graduated with 6 GCE 'O' level subjects. From 16 - 19 years old, Terry attended Moseley Hall Grammar School in Cheadle, Cheshire UK, and graduated with 3 GCE 'A' level subjects.

Terry then engaged in a 5 year apprenticeship program in Manchester with A.V. Roe Aviation to become a qualified Aeronautical/Mechanical Engineer. Upon completion, left A.V. Roe and changed careers completely to Industrial sales as a Technical Representative travelling in Greater Merseyside, North Wales, Cheshire and the

Midlands. During this period got married and lived in Macclesfield, Cheshire.

In 1971, Terry joined the Wynn's Oil Company, selling advanced lubricants to automotive outlets throughout Cheshire, UK on a straight commission basis. However, in 1975, Terry emigrated to Canada with his family and worked for a Wynn's distributor in London, Ontario, as a salesman and was ultimately promoted to Sales Manager. He only worked there 18 months and then quit to start a used car warranty company known as Lubrico Warranty in South Western Ontario.

After almost 43 years, Lubrico was now Canadawide and was sold in January 2020 to an insurance company competitor.

CHAPTER TWO

Developing Connection to Self and Others Fosters Business Growth

By Kristina Kastelanac

I began to feel stagnant in my work. That was my first clue indicating that I had achieved a certain level of success in my practice. I am a Naturopathic Doctor and had been in practice for 9 years when I began to feel this stagnation. I felt that I had reached a certain level of mastery in building my skills as a mind-body focused practitioner; my practice was full, and referrals were occurring regularly. As my business continued to grow, year by year, I continued to receive offers to speak and present, to host workshops, and to share my experiences and knowledge with people looking to re-connect with themselves and their fullest potential.

I also had two little ones through those years, and it was important for me to balance my home life with my work life. I would spend as many hours a week in clinic as I could, until I felt the balance going askew and would rein myself in. It was a constant evaluation and re-evaluation of how I chose to use my time. When I was with my patients, I was fiercely present and supported them in their healing journey. Eventually, I knew that if I worked more hours I would exhaust myself and would not be able to help people in the way that I was meant to. I began to sense the limitations of my energy and my capacity to be fully present in practice. I had to admit to myself that the hours I put in serving people, while being fully present and engaged, were finite. I had hit my own glass ceiling.   I was happy with what I had created over the last 9 years, but I felt this stagnancy tug at me.

What you should know about me is that I work as hard on my own stuff as I do with all of my patients. I have had this insatiable drive to improve myself, to work toward my goals and to achieve success, since childhood. Give it all you've got, go! I think this mentality stemmed from my lineage. I had a grandfather that stood up and said no to a communist regime and was driven out of his homeland, fearing for his life. He drove himself into the ground physically to survive in this world. As a child, I witnessed his drive and determination firsthand.   He was a very quiet man. He suffered in silence and I could feel that suffering as a child. I believe that my grand-parents and parents imparted to me, epi-genetically and through early childhood modeling, that 'you strug-gle, and you search; you work yourself to the bone to survive and you rise again and again'.

After doing much of my own inner work I can clearly state that I do not advocate this as a way that I, or any-one else, should aspire to live their lives. This mindset served my grandfather well in his struggle to survive, but the pattern never broke once he had established a new life in a new country. As a child I watched this pat-tern of survival persist and become highly dysfunctional. It led to a very hard life, with very little capacity for free-dom, joy, and fulfillment.

My grandfather and father knew why they were doing what they were doing. Their core motivations were no-ble and good, and they always shared them with us. They worked hard so we, their children and grandchil-dren, could have a better life than they did. The little, tender being that I was soaked all of that up. I had a strong need in me to comply with their beliefs and I wanted to make them happy and proud. This is what drove me to work hard in school. Thankfully, I found something that I loved to learn about - biology, physiol-ogy and the human body.   I was fascinated by these subjects and my adopted belief of, "work hard, and nev-er stop" was directed toward something that actually stirred my passion and curiosity and brought me joy. I had it all figured out. I knew what I loved, I knew where I wanted to go, and I knew how to get there - dig in and work hard.

Over the years, this trans-generational pattern started to show its imbalance and dysfunction in my own life. I began to notice that the blind motivation of hard work did not always serve me or my family. My world view slowly began to shift with experience. I began to realize that hard work does not always lead to success. I knew that I had to unlearn this belief-pattern, and to be honest, I still have A LOT of growth to do around this realization. At this point in my journey, hard work often equates to an absent-minded habit that continually exhausts me. However, I feel that as I continue to heal this within myself, I indirectly impact my father and grandfather's struggles in a positive way.

So, I acquired their workhorse work ethics. Accompanying this unconscious belief that hard work equals success, I also had this innate urge in me (as most little ones do) to want to ease the suffering of my elders. I wanted to help my grandfather and father to heal, to not feel so much pain. The only way that I knew to do this, at the time, was to obey and follow what they said: study hard, be 'good', be quiet when asked, make something of yourself.

Overall, these early patterns of hard work supported me and helped me attain a certain level of success at school and in my practice. However, once I had a grasp of the basics in my business, this pattern of belief became limiting. It simply created the same suffering and struggle that I saw in my father and grandfather. I soon recognized that I had to build new skills in my practice, such as allowing, letting go, and building patience. If I hoped to be present for my patients and my family in the ways that they needed me to be, this self-reflection and self-development were of the utmost importance. I was "ok" at what I did and how I worked, but I wanted to feel a sense of mastery in my practice! I believe a key to experiencing continuous success is knowing that you need to look at yourself. You need to dig deep into what is holding you back from allowing greater levels of success in your life.

The journey to being able to do this deeper work within myself started early in my life. As a child and a teen, I struggled with chronic sinus infections. As an ND, I have come to know the multitude of influences that can contribute to a chronic state of ill health. I know that my own ill health was partially due to an intolerance to gluten (and possibly most grains). I know it had to do with my father smoking in our home and car while I was growing up. I know that it was also due to the emotional climate of my home. My father struggled while a civil war raged in his home country, and we felt this struggle through his anger, grief and restlessness. These layers of influence overwhelmed my senses. My body defended itself by shutting down the optimal functioning of these senses, most notably my ears and my sinuses. I began to realize that, deep down, the grief and loss that my father and grandfather suffered from having to leave their homeland was being transferred to me, and that my body was trying its best to cope. I also came to realize that part of my struggles stemmed from infancy, and from not feeling attended to by my mother. Like many of us, the list is long, but I do not place blame on any of these relationships or experiences. They are simply facts.

These experiences challenged my body and mind to find ways to tolerate and sequester them, so that I could function in this world as a young child. My body did so by holding on to these things, lending to chronic sinus infections.

Along with these early childhood challenges I carried a deep "knowing" that my body and mind could heal. I knew, and still know now, that all of us have this ability to heal ourselves. However, this deep-seated knowledge was challenged when the chronic sinus infections began. As a little girl I bargained with God: "I will be really good if you just take this pain away." Most days it was so intolerable that I just wanted to cut my nose off.

These infections were what prompted me to dive deep within myself. It made me ask questions, as early as the age of 10. It made me search for answers throughout my early life. I had this knowing deep within me, that I would figure out the root cause and help my body to heal. I am sure that I would not be in the healing profession if I did not have those early experiences of pain and suffering, that proverbial pebble in my shoe. In my work today, I aspire to encourage people to understand that they have a capacity to heal. It is my purpose to support people through this process, and I know that my own suffering and struggle drove me to become a Naturopathic Doctor.

In my training as an ND I learned many modalities to help slowly uncover these patterns, but one modality in particular taught me how to listen to my body in a very deep and profound way. I learned how to track my bodily sensations and to grow my level of capacity to tolerate the intense emotions and sensations that my body was holding onto. As I unpacked these patterns, the weight came off, and the triggers and hardships of life felt much easier to move through.

As a result, I've been able to see first-hand how internal patterns can hold us back from achieving continuous success, from feeling fulfilled and truly being supportive to others. It was the fear lodged in my body, layer by layer, that prevented me from living a life of joy, presence and calm. Through my own internal work, I continually uncover layers within myself. As I gently work through these layers, I feel that I am able to consistently reach new heights in my approach to my relationships and to my business.

So after 9 years of practice, as I witnessed this nagging feeling of stagnancy build within me, I knew that my approach needed something more. I knew that this was an internal prompt telling me that I needed to expand my business. This new business idea that began to percolate was not only for the benefit of others. By moving forward into a new venture, I would also have the opportunity to continue to do my own internal work and to heal newly uncovered layers.

I threw myself into a new and very inspiring project. I developed an online program, and was going to spread the word! I was going to help everyone that wanted to heal their body, from the inside out! Or, so I thought. I put my feet to pavement and grinded out this program. I began the rollercoaster ride of learning how to build a website, market an online program and do all that you are 'supposed' to do on social media. I spent many hours away from my husband and two girls to get it all done. I worked hard and my grandfather would have been proud. Guess what? I felt like a complete failure. Only a few people signed up for the first launch, and again, very few for the second launch. It crushed me and it showed me that hard work alone DOES NOT bring success. I had to dig deeper. I knew that I needed to build my capacity for patience and for persistence; success isn't immediate. I also began to realize that I was missing something significant and that I could not do this alone. I needed a community of support. I only realized this once the universe presented me with a very scary, but curious opportunity.

I was introduced to a group of likeminded female entrepreneurs, led by a woman that I admire and trust,
who were forming a year-long mastermind class. I sat
with the idea of joining them, and it terrified me. As I
uncovered the fear around joining this community, I
was led to revisit patterns that were relayed to me, both
consciously and unconsciously, during childhood. A
deep mistrust of community rose up in me and, as I unpacked this within myself, I realized that it stemmed
from my grandfather's experience of betrayal and per-
secution at the hands of communism. Could I trust a
community to support me, to really be there for me, or
would they burn me in the end? I was at a crossroads. I
could choose to renegotiate this fear and to heal the
patterns of my grandfather's past, or I could choose to
keep small, letting this online project dwindle and die. I
chose to dive in and embrace this community. This decision quickly revealed something to me. It sparked a
deep understanding about the importance of connection, and of having the 'right support network' in place,
of being part of a healthy, helpful community.

Through connection and support I have come to further
realize what it means to be successful, happy and balanced in the work that I do. In order to foster true and
lasting success in business, there are 3 vital elements
that must be nurtured and considered:

1) We need a community of support

2) we need a persistent and patient urge/motivation within us, despite the obstacles that inevitably arise

3) we need to take ownership of the patterns and beliefs that hold us back and that need to change, so that we can continually improve, adjust and optimize our actions.

We need all of these elements to help us and our businesses grow.

When I contemplate success, my success, the first thing that I think about is all of the effort made; all the dedication, late nights, early mornings, struggles and sacrifices. Then, I think about the gifts I innately have and the thoughts/behaviours/skills that I have fostered so that they have become my strengths. These internal resources are all essential for us to manifest success, but we must go deeper and ask the questions: what allowed us to develop these skills? How did we find the time and energy to focus on and cultivate them? How did the opportunity present itself to help us to build success? In short, what external resources made it possible for us to do this work?

It is just as important to foster our internal resources as it is to acknowledge our external resources. We need a community of family and friends, colleagues and connections to support and foster this growth. Our community and connections allow for opportunity to arrive, and these opportunities allow us to develop our strengths so that we all benefit.   For example, I acknowledge that there are certain external structures that allowed me to become a Naturopathic Doctor (i.e. Naturopathy is a fully regulated profession where I live, and it is a profession dominated by women).   Had my father chosen to remain in a war torn, eastern European country, I likely would not be where I am today because the structures would not have been there for me in the same way.

Oftentimes, the external structures and influences that create our limiting beliefs are the very same external resources that allow us the opportunity to grow and heal. For example, I had to renegotiate the limiting belief that hard work and suffering are the only way to survive and that joy and self-actualization are not achievable. However, it was that very same hard work and suffering, endured by my grandfather and father, which allowed me the material comfort to pursue my dreams and heal my own wounds.

Through all of the healing work that I have witnessed, both clinically and personally, it has become clear to me that we all have layers of struggle, this deep suffering, that occurs along the way. We all have the light within us, but not all of us have the external support to foster its growth. We may have a number of internal resources and strengths, but we need external supports that may or may not be available to us. If there are enough internal and external resources, then we have what it takes to address these layers of struggle. We can begin to climb out from under the heavy weight of our limiting beliefs and behavioural patterns, giving ourselves the opportunity to succeed at what we set our sights on.

This perspective guides us to look deep within ourselves, but also to step outside of ourselves and into gratitude. From gratitude we can cultivate trust. From trust we can cultivate connection (both internal and external). From connection we can cultivate a feeling of safety and happiness, and from happiness we can step confidently into our purpose and passion in this life. As business owners we are asked to do our own internal work; to lead with our hearts, to connect with those whom we serve, to acknowledge our limitations and to ask for support when we need it. Your work is the work of all those who came before you, the work of those that you surround yourself with now, and it is the work of your highest self.

As I continue to do my own work, it has become clear that my purpose and my wildest dream is to guide and witness people as they renegotiate their limiting beliefs and nervous system patterns. By working through the stuck patterns that we all hold onto physically, mentally and emotionally, we create the opportunity to reconnect to ourselves and to our fullest potentials.

Then a Pandemic Hits

How to Begin Again, After a Crisis

Crisis affects all of us at some point in our lives, both personally and professionally. It is a fundamental experience of life. We rise and we fall and hopefully we rise again. Our businesses are not immune to the impact of crisis. I have spent many hours reflecting on the COVID-19 pandemic and I have come to recognize 3 lessons that I needed to learn, so that I could begin again in the wake of major world events. I wish to share them with you here, in the hopes that they might support you as you rise in to the new, again.

My first lesson is about the importance of observing where the world is headed and working toward incorporating these changes in your business. It was obvious where the world was headed regarding online services and technology. I could see the importance that technology held in my business. We benefited from the basic uses of our computer and debit/credit machine in our business daily, but I knew I needed to automate things further. I needed to greet technology and work with it to help grow my business, instead of avoiding it and hoping that I wouldn't have to change. I tend to delay or avoid making changes to my business when it is new and foreign to me, and when I am not strong in that particular skill. As most of us do, I tend to procrastinate on the implementation of things I know little about; things that would require a lot of extra time and energy to learn and then implement. Perhaps outsourcing, or delegating, could have been an option here, if we weren't in the middle of this crisis and cashflow was not virtually at a halt. I now recognize how crucial it was to put these things in place as I saw them arise, and face my fear and avoidance of the new and different. If I had taken the initiative earlier maybe I would have been able to delegate and seek support. This was an important lesson for me. As this crisis hit I had to take the time and put in the effort to implement all these tech pieces that I was avoiding. I knew it was good for my business to do this, but I just allowed myself to ignore it for so long.

I have learned, in a very tangible way, that those areas of our business that we least want to explore, or change, are likely what we need to look at more closely. By examining the nooks and crannies that we tend to avoid and ignore in our business (both consciously and unconsciously), we begin to expand our awareness. We become aware of our limiting beliefs and processes, and we invite the possibility of finding new solutions and better ways of working. By staring technology in the face, I am developing new systems. For example, I am beginning to implement e-filing vs. paper files. We are now moving to an online dispensary, where patients can continue to receive their herbal and supplement support and don't need to come into the clinic to do so, while limiting the burden of carrying inventory. We now have virtual visits available to patients on secure platforms and are using a system that can host the virtual files, carry out the virtual visits and automate scheduling and payment. Now that we are finally implementing all of these changes and we see how these benefit our business, I recognize how much fear holds me back from making progress in my business. I am truly thankful for this lesson and as I move forward I will set aside time and space to truly face what needs to change instead of succumbing to the overwhelm that change brings. I commit to examining, and re-examining those aspects of my business that I would much rather ignore, but no longer can.

The second lesson I learned through this current crisis is about financial preparedness. I feel like in life we all just get caught up in the day-to-day responsibilities of our businesses and of our lives, especially if we have a young family with little ones, full-time work, and new projects we wish to develop. I recognize I did not take the time needed to look more deeply at cashflow vs. what we were saving. I relied on cashflow to carry us along and cover all our incoming expenses. Of course, that all worked, as long as we could keep providing care to our patients. Through this crisis where we were unable to provide care, it has now become very clear that we need enough in our accounts to cover all our typical monthly expenses for at least 3 months. I also recognized the need to keep evaluating our budget and make those adjustments more frequently.

Lastly, and likely the most important lesson I learned through this crisis, is that taking care of myself is crucial to my business. Slowing down allowed for an introspective journey to unfold. The quieting of the day-to-day rigours of business facilitated a deeper capacity for me to stay present to the demands at hand. It became clear, in a deeper way, that self-development is more about being than it is about doing. The more that I develop my ability to be, the better decisions I will make and the more productive and efficient I can become. If I can be present, maintain focus and encourage connection and openness in my relationships with patients, colleagues and staff, the less confusion and fewer misunderstandings there will be amongst them. This crisis continues to affirm for me the importance of addressing my inner patterns of fear, anger and worry that continually show up. As I address them, my business and my work relationships greatly benefit.

This journey has also re-affirmed for me what is truly important in life: that health and community are deeply important, that all our businesses impact one another, and that deep down, even though my business appears to play a small role, it is a crucial one, as is each and every other business. Like an ecosystem or a living organism, we all matter and influence one another. It is our job to make sure our influence is loving and expansive. With that I vow to continue to nurture my own growth and healing and witness the impact it has in my life, in my business, and perhaps to witness how this trickles down to other people and businesses that I am connected to.

About the Author

Kristina Kastelanac BHSc., ND, SEP is a Naturopathic Doctor and clinic co-owner of the Village Naturopathic Clinic in London, Canada, where she has been serving her community since 2010. She considers the core naturopathic principles of "treat the root cause", and "the healing power of nature", as guideposts on her journey to discover what best supports those she serves.

Kristina sees the body as a powerful web of interconnected systems functioning on many levels (the physical, mental, emotional and energetic). She views symptoms as the body's way to communicate with us. She listens to the body's story and invites others to do the same. In her experience, the body is capable of great healing, when given the right conditions to do so.

Connect with Kristina:

ND Practice: https://www.villagenaturopaths.com

Facebook Village Naturopathic Clinic:
https://www.facebook.com/villagenaturopathic

CHAPTER THREE

And Yet? A Tale of Two Choices

By Kate Thompson

"There is a time for everything, and a season for every activity under the heavens.....a time to tear down and a time to build." Ecclesiastes 3:1,3

The numbers, the goals - what's next? I'm at a business retreat, ready to learn. Anticipating and open to new possibilities.

Mapping it out – business is stable. As a Certified Financial Planner, there has been consistent growth each year. Efficiencies have been implemented. Referrals are good. My personal cash flow is better than I ever expected I could achieve. We have enough, more than enough. As a result, we enjoy being generous and look for ways to support our community and church. There is much to be very thankful for.

And yet.

What about that other dream? The idea that I would have my own space – my own business – literally my name outside on the road. Ever since I was young I had dreamed it would happen. Not because my name was that important or out of a puffed-up ego on my part, but my own knowing that it was meant to happen eventually. For what? I wasn't quite clear on that yet, but I suspected there was more waiting before I'd find out.

Faced with the possibility that I could be living smaller – more carefully – than I should, what else might be possible?

My current working arrangement gave me the freedom I needed. No quotas, per se. No one breathing down my neck or telling me what to sell. The drawback was there was no collaboration either – or opportunities to share a vision or affect any real changes. An annual, semi-annual or occasional check-in and 'talk to you later' was the extent of our collaboration.

I am grateful all the same. Don't mistake that. This arrangement was a decade in the making and I was given an opportunity when I needed it. A previous business partnership had unexpectedly blown up and I was vulnerable and hurt and this was a good, safe space.

This contract was the right fit. I was a hard worker and producer. I provided efforts they needed and I thought there would be a space where my personality and drive could be an asset to them, for me and, most importantly, for our clients.

As an all-in kind of person, I doubled up on meetings and kept a relentless schedule. I did more than I thought possible. Nights in hotels. Late meetings. Hours on the highways. Endless expectations with 150% effort given by myself. It was self-imposed but I realize now that it was also externally imposed. I had something to prove to myself but also to the industry. Regardless of the changes made over the past 25 years, there still aren't many high-producing, independent female advisors in our business. I have learned in these past years how to bring myself to the client relationship and connect in a way that I had not authentically experienced before. In short, I found my voice. I loved the connections. The opportunity to help. To be counted on. To create space for peace – to alleviate stress – to encourage.

The business thrived as a result. Not because I'm particularly smart or dazzling.

The thing is I love working! I love thinking about people and their families and helping them imagine and work out their finances. Interestingly enough, it has been this past year's journey that has helped me to really know this. It's simply not just "work". It's a real honor and pleasure to be in people's homes or at my office spending time getting to the heart of their "money stuff". Helping them figure out what to do next, then what's next after that, and so on. I love taking on what is overwhelming, unanticipated, or out of control and making it manageable—and if possible, also having a bit of fun in the process.

Money questions arise for most people at some point in their lives. Not enough. Too much. Big decisions about careers, dreams, and expectations.

There are endless opportunities for me to come alongside and help. Sometimes it might be more of a nudge. Other times it is offering clarity around decisions to be made, or it's a 'give-it-all-to-me-and-we-are-going-to-rebuild-this together' sort of situation.

Simple or complicated. One-off meetings or decades of time together. It is all a real pleasure.

So, now I am 10 years into the chance to be part of many people's lives in this particular practice. Things are great – not perfect – but from all outside measurable markers, it has been very successful and I'm evaluating the year. I'm looking at all the responsibilities I'm carrying and can't figure out why I'm not as happy as I thought or think I should be.

What's this all about then?

Why not?

Am I inherently ungrateful? No.

Am I not satisfied? No.

Maybe I'm just so driven I can't stop? Actually, that's not it either.

In a business reflection exercise, I was to write down what a typical week looked like. On a huge presentation paper, I started jotting down items: dealing with emails, follow-ups, team meetings, family stuff, reading, self-care... it went on and on until I filled the page, and I still wasn't done! Mostly complete, I presented my page to the group and then saw the reactions. It was a powerful and humbling moment when I realized that the visual of "my typical day" simply communicated that I was exhausted. My responsibilities, this overload, had felt pretty "normal" to me until then. I suspected it would slow down once I figured out a really good time management system - this seems just a little absurd now. By taking in an outside reaction to the presentation of my day, I realized it was time to make changes.

I was exhausted and I normalized it. It was expected. What could change? Was anything else possible? I was paralyzed at the realization that doing life any differently seemed impossible. I was incapable of making any changes or even making a decision.

But what could I do differently? Would I dare to dream it was possible to want something else?

Would I let people down in the process? This was an intolerable option. I felt trapped. Not in the work, and not by the clients, but in the lack of choice or ability to have things another way or to consider saying no.

I realized that I had said yes to almost every opportunity or request that came along. 'Yes' meant I care about you. 'Yes' meant I am accepting what is "given to me". 'Yes' meant I am grateful. I am a good person. I am kind. I care. 'Yes' got pretty screwed up in my head.

'No' was never an option. It was wrong, negative. 'No' meant 'rejection'.

Logically I knew all of this was nonsense, but logic wasn't in control at this point.

> *"What stands in the way, becomes the way"*
> *– Marcus Aurelius*

Many of us have a voice inside us desiring to please others. It is looking for ways to avoid making others angry. It is the not-so-silent accuser of, "you are not good enough". And in the moments when we scream, "No more please, I'm so tired!", the voice marches on with the rally, "You must! If you don't it will be disastrous, horrendous! Just keep going."

Now, there are seasons to rally. Times to dig in because things are tough. Marriages fail. Jobs end. Kids need us. We do what we must and we drive on – it can be so very motivating. It can produce very good results.

But sometimes a season becomes years and years turn into decades. Then it becomes extreme forever, a continuously pulsing "gotta". Never, never stopping because you must work harder – you must push longer. You will be better only when you give more. EFFORT = results. Results are approval. Approval means peace. Spending time in my head through this exercise was not a comfortable experience.

I had a choice. I was challenged with the idea that there was no wrong answer.

What? Was that even possible? No wrong answer? What about black and white? Right or wrong? Pass or fail? Woah! I was in deep trouble. And I was frozen, transfixed by fear. I hated it.

I knew then that If I wanted anything to change it was going to need to be a radical, all-encompassing move. Something DARING.

Don't get me wrong. I don't run a major corporation. My life does not have worldwide significance. There wasn't going to be a tweet blast depending on what I chose. But to me, it was earth-shattering. I was stuck in the decision process, and that in and of itself was a strong indication that something was very wrong.

I'd faced plenty of hard stuff over the years. I knew how to work out a tough spot and get a plan together. Why was this so hard?

So, I chose change.

I made a decision. I made a commitment to something unknown and cried with the relief of choosing.

You would think then that the plan flowed, and that I had amazing inspiration and energy. Clarity, perhaps?

No. I sat on this decision for 4 months! I Evaluated. Questioned. Re-evaluated. Dismissed. Weighed out all the pros and cons. I tried to talk myself out of it. Rationalized and realized every fear until I was sick of debating it.

And yet, even with all of this, still there was a spark. A new confidence. An excited expectation I'd not yet experienced.

The possibility of something new brought with it all kinds of possibilities – dreams.

It didn't seem worthwhile to take on new risks or to make changes without also considering what else could happen – what possibilities for expansion were possible to support our community and equip clients and partners.

Being fairly pragmatic I knew that the grass was not greener and that new challenges would come up, so I was prepared mentally. What I didn't expect was what would happen to me physically in this process.

As I experienced new levels of excitement about the future – frankly realizing how much tension and pressure I had been under for so long - my body had a new response. The years of stress had taken their toll on me. I'd had stomach issues consisting of intestinal irritations and chronic flare-ups. I'd had a long-term inability to sleep. I managed as best I could with prayer, supports, and diet, but it was always a moving target. No gluten helped for a while. No carbs. No alcohol. I did years of long-distance running. Counseling. Meditation. Dancing. Yoga. So much trying and searching. All solutions helped for the short-term, but no major impact was made. Until now.

"Normal is an illusion. What is normal for the spider is
chaos for the fly."
– Charles Addams

The first episode (which we have come to call them) happened after a very good and long week. After a particularly great week. I had not yet had "the conversation" at work, but I knew it would happen soon. I was rehearsing it all the time. This particular day, though, was spent doing what we all loved most - encouraging friends. I felt such gratitude for the time to do so, and was dreaming of the possibility of having more space for this in my new business.

And then it happened. My body shut down. I couldn't move or speak or snap out of it. It was an absurd reaction, happening suddenly and lasting for hours. We had an emergency visit with no answers. Test after test. I had not had something toxic. I did not have heart problems. I had not had a stroke. I was just simply immobile. Frozen. I thought perhaps I was dying. And in those long hours, I came to realize that I wasn't. I had a good long stretch to think. Pray. Face profound fear and allow it to pass. I came out of it slowly. The first day I rested. The second day I rested. My calendar was cleared. I was paying attention now. It forced me to a place of re-evaluation. Was I on the wrong track? Was there a sign I had missed along the way? What had I ignored? What had I done wrong? Or what if I was actually on the right track? Was it possible that I was just not accustomed to this kind of space and peace? Was it so foreign to my body that it did not know how to respond? Had I been living numbly for so long that this really produced such a dramatic response? I believed so.

This change had challenged my system and now it was time to really be brave. And so I continued to rest. Pray. Regain my strength and then keep on. I knew with certainty after this time of recovery that I was on the right path. I was doing the opposite of what I had done for so long to make a new way for myself.

This was not done on my own, though. I received help from supportive experts and learned so much. I took the time I needed to listen to my body for the first time in my adult life. I've had a few more episodes where I have experienced similar shut-downs since, but thankfully they've always happened at home. Usually after a peak time of stress, they weren't as scary and have passed more quickly. It was becoming an indicator of when I had pushed too hard. I willingly listened and adjusted as needed. This experience has provided me with incredible clarity and respect for my body. For decades I had spent so much time in my head, pushing myself and ignoring my own needs. This continues to be a learning experience for me. It's not an easy lesson, but the journey has been exciting as new possibilities pop up.

And so, with a gentler drive, an acceptance of a limited physical body, and with so much humility, I pursued the next steps to make the business change.

To say it all has been easy would be false. There were disappointments along the way. But then we can't make everyone happy all the time. Facing that fact was difficult and required massive resiliency. Allowing others to respond in the way that they wanted, leaving space for misunderstandings, and accepting the fact that sometimes people say yes and mean no, have all been required of me. Finishing well doesn't always mean finishing based on your own definition of the word. It is doing the best you can with what you've got and letting that be enough. This was very tough.

And so with terms negotiated, offers accepted and a date set, contracts were changed, space was found, and everything for it.

In retrospect, it was a massive to-do list that was fairly easily executed once I got started with the right perspective. Less drive, more ease. I still had lots of lists, but was working through them with more faith. Slowing down in the decision-making. When it was becoming overwhelming, I was simply stopping until I had full energy to move ahead.

What took the most time and energy was developing a new vision.

Creating a business versus running a solo practice is a whole new thing. I could have taken what I was already doing, moved to new space and kept on the same track. That in and of itself would have been a success. But why change without first examining and determining what should stay, and dreaming about what might be?

Now, this was fun. What about my business could be shared? Was mentorship an option? Could the business be reproduced? Expanded? Could there be a way to encourage and support others in my field? Could I help them serve their clients better? Could I be generous with sharing resources? Space? Were there other ministries we could support with our money, and also with our time? Could we create a community for others to learn and grow in, to the point where they were financially stable and inspired, equipped, to give back to our community? 'What else' became a very exciting conversation. Poster boards and vision statements articulated our new rally cry. The idea that "we are all wealthy" was born. We have more than we need, more than the average person worldwide. It may be in cash or in opportunity, gifts, and potential. If we can move beyond a scarcity & fear mentality, so much is possible.

It was no longer about 'when' or 'if', but about 'why not?'. This musing and writing and collaborating kept on through the many months it took to make the actual transition.

Then my focus was on how many people should be on the team. The number was four. I always knew that. Figuring out who these four should be was a much harder exercise. There was a little heartbreak when it came to this experience. Initially, I was so sure I knew who it would be - I was creating job descriptions & developing compensation structures that I thought would be generous.

I was wrong, and I kept on hoping that it would change. The old habit of not wanting anyone to be disappointed was a battle.

Each person that I imagined did not actually happen. The three people I was so sure about turned into three I had not expected. The team we have today is equipped, excited, and a huge blessing. But in those first months, huge fears rose up with the uncertainty and I hated working through it.

I realized through reflection and gentle patience with myself that sometimes "no" today is the best "yes" for the future, particularly given the direction I dreamed we would work towards. Today, as I see everyone together, I experience a new lightness and enthusiasm and I trust that this was the right outcome for everyone.

I am prepared that more of these defining, scary moments may come up as I plan for the next stages of the business. I dream and create based on what I see ahead, and what seems obvious to tackle, or in need of fixing. Now I am also mindful that I may need to head left when right becomes a default.

I am deeply thankful for the many lessons I have learned through this journey. I've made new friends who have cheered me on and who have also challenged me. We have received many loving messages with words from old friends, clients, and family. It was an unexpected gift.

Breaking up is hard to do and I've not experienced anything but deep trauma in the process up until now. The unknown of it, the total fear, has been faced and overcome. I did it, but not on my own. I've had so much help and support and many moments of prayer for wisdom and strength.

As I reflect back on the challenge of change, I see that this is only one part of the journey. The other side of this coin has given rise to a new sense of adventure. The unknown and all its possibilities. Knowing that our team, together, can serve and provide for our clients in a way I never could on my own. This bubbles up such freedom and expectation for myself and for my family. If I'm not exhausted, how much more is possible? Where else could we go? How else might we serve and give? Who else could we encourage to live more fully? Oh, the wonder of it all.

Then a Pandemic Hits

If I had to start all over again, what would I do differently? Lessons learned during a pandemic.

Start sooner. The vision was clear, the timing was negotiable. I should not have given away my time but should have moved forward with a greater sense of urgency. This, of course, is based on my knowledge a major world crisis would happen within 6 months of starting a new direction in my practice. Hindsight is perfect, so I also refuse to beat myself up about it. I have no regrets. I know there was much to learn in the space and time it took me to get where I am now. But, if I had a choice, I would have chosen sooner. Sooner would have given seasons to establish our team and our rhythms and to work out the kinks vs. doing all these things AND coping with a crisis. It's been a massive learning curve and an opportunity to let go of things that held me back. The 'what if's' and the 'worst-case scenarios' never included THIS, and yet here we are. Still standing. Still working.

Moving along. Doing our best and facing the daily changes and challenges. We are much stronger than we think we are. Those notions are nothing now; a wisp compared with what we are dealing with. And yet here we remain. Not knowing what will happen next month, heck - next week. Tomorrow brings us to now. And today is fine even with all its messiness. So we rally, encourage, and count our blessings.

The power of the group or maybe just one or two. Taking bold steps is a great idea. Of course, as leaders we dream of the possibilities, but executing them is another matter. Accepting that my own perfectionist tendencies might be holding me back too much was a humbling exercise. Realizing that the over-analyzing and "prudent" planning could actually perpetuate my "failure is not an option" has given me the opportunity to practice being a little less than perfect and enjoy the result. The thing is, when you let go and allow things to flow, it can be quite beautiful. Natural. And it allows others to do the same. Being a little freer from perfectionism has given rise to new energy and great capacity. Letting go has proven to be an incredibly good thing. This lesson did not come to me naturally. Not one bit. When you have been in the same role for a long time, you hone your skill, have your own efficiencies and preferences (aka you're a control freak), and it seems improbable that another way is possible. Now, enter a group of fabulously enthusiastic and successful business leaders who get to know one other, build trust and empathy, and change will happen. Being part of a small masterclass has allowed me space to be vulnerable and admit when I was stuck. Scared. Maybe even feeling a tiny bit over my head (what? really? no! you too?!) They also gave me space to celebrate. Pause. Really enjoy what I have spent so much time working for. I realize that with the support of a group of good people, you can get through so much more tough stuff. If you want to change, grow and really take hold of that dream, get a gang of believers to walk the road with you. It's amazing to see what happens when you grow and learn and lean in together. If a group is not your thing, and to be honest I would have said it was not mine to start with, find a mentor. Someone who understands you, respects your values and will be bold in speaking out truth in love for what matters most. This person should also be willing to be transparent (we need real people to do real life) and should have their own accomplishments – either personal or in business - by which to relate and empathize with your own desires.

Know your voice. We each have one. Some are quiet. Others are bold. Many are sweet. Some are brash. How we use our voice is up to us. Will you build others up or tear them down? Will you speak out and encourage or say nothing at all? The last few months have forced me to speak up in new ways and do some tough stuff. Things I wouldn't have imagined have happened. Really, would we have dreamed we would have a season (maybe more, we do not know yet) of social distancing, months at home, unable to go out and see clients? Faced with a literal shutdown of most things we take for granted has forced a real examination of what really matters and frankly, what is optional. Our business was deemed essential. But how to function was not spelled out. Faced with markets falling, people afraid, jobs completely turned upside-down, kids at home and no end in sight, there have been some hard days for everyone. During this time many have had to face the possibility that their business just might not exist any longer. The reality is daunting and can cause many to wonder, "Am I next?"

Uncertainty and fear can be contagious. Life is uncertain and unpredictable. This has been a time of realizing that, and for some of us for the very first time. Living in the country we do at this time has not equipped us for quite so much change. We have been able to take control and make effective change for ourselves and our families (with effort) but it's been possible. We are privileged. We have safety nets and we have options. No question. This season has rocked so many of us. Admittedly, it has rocked me as well. I have had my moments of paralyzing fear (enter the power of a good mentor here) and uncertainty about how to serve or what needed to change. Some hard decisions have been made too. Projects were dumped and priorities changed. Pivot has become the word of the year. We all might just be a little dizzy from the whiplash. We, like many, have evaluated our core business and wondered if the problems we solve for clients are still relevant. Entering this time of uncertainty with clients has been clarifying in focus as to what matters most. We realize that coming alongside our clients during the good times is a joy and during the hard times a privilege. The need for a voice of calm reassurance has never been greater and is not going to stop.

Admittedly it has taken the shake-up of this crisis for me to understand the true need of my own voice - to call out to others and be ready when they in turn call back.

When life is flipped upside down, I have the tendency to think everything needs to be re-evaluated. It is an approach that does help to consider new things and dream bigger dreams; however, in moments of overwhelm it can be an exhausting, scattering practice. I am grateful for the time we spent as a team to dream of and write out our values and mission. It has provided confidence to rein in the hard days and press on. Our focus and goals expressed in a few short words and phrases have allowed us to know deeply who we are and why we do what we do. The lesson learned was not to underestimate the power of your company's passion and vision. Remember why you started in the first place, be brave enough to ask yourself if that need still exists, and if so, press on!

About the Author

Kate Thompson's career as a Certified Financial Planner has a humble beginning. Struggling to provide for her two kids as a single mum there was often more month than money. She realized that she needed to truly learn how money works and how use a budget. These life experiences catapulted her into a time of deep learning about money management and financial stewardship. Now, with over 25 years experience in the financial planning industry, it remains her passion to help others make wise decisions with what they earn, to live below their means and become exponential savers and givers. Her ability to coach people with their money is, at its core, a relationship – always evolving, changing and growing. Kate, along with her husband, four children and two granddaughters, lives in London, Ontario where she has volunteered for numerous years with local non-profits that share her love for others.

Connect with Kate:

https://rockthompson.ca

CHAPTER FOUR

How Not to be an Asshole

By Anita Watkins

"When we are no longer able to change a situation, we are challenged to change ourselves.
Everything can be taken from a man but one thing: the last of the human freedoms—to choose one's attitude in any given set of circumstances, to choose one's own way. Between stimulus and response there is a space. In that space is our power to choose our response. In our response lies our growth and our freedom."
-Viktor Frankl Man's Search for Meaning

I'm pretty sure my parents would not approve of the title of this chapter, but I know that they would completely support everything I am about to share. The reason is simple: it is the foundation of my youth.

My parents were immigrants, and as a child of immigrants, their values were the core of my own beliefs.

Hard work, empathy, and self-reliance but a duty to help others were all the foundation of my youth. Of course, I had to put my own spin on it.

Don't be an asshole. I think that is really the secret to success. Now don't judge me too quickly (don't be an asshole...see what I did there?) because I think you will see by the end of this chapter that there is a truth to this philosophy.

1) Don't be an asshole to yourself.

I thought I would start with the hardest one of all, because if you don't master this, the rest will be really challenging. We all have that voice in our heads that is the devil's advocate, the naysayer and the asshole. In some ways, that voice can be helpful as it alerts us to potential weaknesses in our ideas and plans.

I don't want to suggest that it is always bad to listen to this voice. As a teacher, this voice helped me plan multiple contingencies into my lessons so that classroom management was rarely an issue for me.

As a parent, this voice helped to smooth down those inevitable bumps in the road. The travel loot bag emerged from that voice. Our parents all lived a full day's drive from us so we often took our three children on the road to see them. Listening to that voice resulted in the invention of the travel loot bag. I would prepare a bag of treats, snacks and toys for each child. They didn't get to see them until they were safely strapped in the car. Then the fun would begin! For the whole trip, they were in charge of their own entertainment. It was a brilliant strategy that I thank that voice for helping me to create.

As a business owner, it allows me to quickly pivot when a strategy is not working. That voice can be a lifesaver.

The problem occurs when we give this voice the main stage in our lives. It is meant to be in the backseat. In fact, sometimes it should even go in the trunk. It should not be allowed to take the main stage. Ever.

The main stage is reserved for the voice of hope, optimism and courage. It is the voice of joy and vision that gives our lives the best chance of rising to the level that we yearn to. This is the voice that allows us to dream big. It is the voice that allows us to see the potential in ourselves. It is the voice that lifts others along with us.

When we give that voice the main stage, nothing can stop us.

Making the decision to change careers from teaching to business owner in mid-life would have been the perfect time to let the asshole brain take over. It was present. No question. I would have been stupid to ignore the messages it was sending me. Those messages were LOUD AND CLEAR:

What will people think? Will my family understand? What am I doing, thinking about leaving a secure job and income in favor of the complete unknown? Will I risk my pension? Who am I to think that I have the talent to earn a living taking photographs? Who am I to think that I have the skills to run a business? Who am I to think that I can make this work?

These are all valid points. And I addressed them all. But I chose to listen to the other voices in my head that had other ideas.

Who cares what people think? I never have before. My family loves me because of who I am, not because of what I do. Decisions are often reversible. If it doesn't work out, I can always go back to teaching. I am smart enough, or know people that are smart enough, to fig- ure out the financial consequences of this decision. Tal- ent is not as important as the willingness to learn. I can learn the skills needed to run a business. What I am not good at, or don't want to do, I can hire people to do. I am exactly the person that can make this work. That is the voice I chose to give the center stage to.

2) Don't let your instincts be assholes.

Your instincts can be assholes in disguise. How many times have you made assumptions about another per- son's intentions and had this come to bite you in the ass?

I had a student once in a class for high-risk kids. He was normally in a pretty good mood and an enthusiastic student in class.

One day, he was being a complete asshole. He was snapping at people, rude, impatient, and definitely a dis- traction in class. I know many of my colleagues might have just sent him to the office. I chose another tactic.

As the students were working on something, I went over to him and crouched down so that we could have a private conversation. I told him that it was clear he wasn't himself and asked what was up. He looked at me with complete relief at being asked and shared with me that the home next to his had been on fire that night, and that between the noise and the lights of the fire-trucks that were flashing into his bedroom all night he just didn't get much sleep. He was exhausted.

All I could think of was how grateful I was that in spite of his night from hell, he still CHOSE to come to my class. That he felt safe enough to come into my space and process the night he'd had.

He apologized for his behavior and, feeling heard and cared for, settled into a productive and respectful routine.

I was so grateful that I had chosen to assume good intentions.

Assume

Good

Intentions

That is some of the best advice I have ever gotten. In fact, it got me my first teaching job.

I was being interviewed for a full-time contract teaching position right after I finished teacher's college. It was in a school with a great reputation in a time when teaching jobs were scarce. I was nervous.

The interview was going well but I wasn't feeling like they were all in. I knew that they were interviewing many candidates for the job. Then the crucial question was asked: what would I do if a student called me a bitch?

I still do not know where I got the guts to do this, but I went immediately with my instincts. Instead of a well-crafted answer about discipline and the different strategies I could implement, I simply stated: it would depend on if I was being one.

That was the moment that everything shifted in the interview and I am certain I got the job because of this. It was a clever response, but I meant it with all sincerity. Because, if I was being a bitch and treating students with a lack of respect in that moment, I would have to own it and deal with the situation accordingly. If I wasn't being a bitch, then clearly the student was acting out and I would have to support them in a different way.

By assuming good intentions, I got my first job.

My mother was a woman of grace, empathy and compassion. Her life was incredibly difficult. Her father was stolen by the Soviets to fight in the army in WWII. She was only 3 years old. Her mother took her three children, all of whom were under the age of five, and ran from Lithuania to Poland. Changing their identities, they were able to create a life for themselves in communist Poland. In spite of this, she was a master of this ability to assume good intentions. With her empathy and fierce conviction that good triumphs over evil, she lived her life assuming that others had good intentions. She wanted to see the best in people, and she did.

The interesting thing I have discovered is that if you believe in the best in humanity, people will often rise to that expectation. My mother ended up working in the first Women in Crisis Center in Sault Ste. Marie, Canada. There she was able to use her high expectations of people, along with her ability to see the best in people, to change lives. There was a fierceness in her conviction. She did it with all her heart. I know many women and their children owe her a deep debt of gratitude.

I often hear my mom's voice in my head when I look at a situation now. She taught me the skill to reframe. Instead of assuming what the other person intended, my mom taught me to imagine, with empathy, what else that person might be experiencing that was causing them to act that way. The reality is that people rarely have the energy or inclination to intentionally cause us grief. It is usually an unintended consequence of their personal circumstances.

3) Don't be an asshole to the people you love.

I guess this one seems the most obvious one of all, but I think it is one we tend to fail at frequently.

My father died before my wedding, but I did get to hear him speak at my sister's wedding. He was an articulate man who really enjoyed public speaking. But what impressed me the most was the fact that THIS was the speech he chose to keep short. I often thought about why he did that. It was so unlike him in many ways. But I think the reason he chose to do that was that he wanted his message to be clear and remembered. And it was. His message was simple. For a long and successful relationship, you have to choose to never take each other for granted.

Never Take Each Other For Granted

I really believe that this is the answer to successful relationships of all kinds.

We seem to expend so much of our energy to be seen, to be loved, and to get attention from others, at the expense of the relationships we actually hold the closest to our hearts. Are we impatient with the ones we love? Do we sit back and expect them to read our minds? Do we neglect to show them through our words and actions how much we appreciate them and love them? And then we are surprised that our most important relationships are at risk.

This is true in our business relationships too. Our best clients are often the ones that are the easiest to work with. There is an ease and effortlessness in those relationships that makes those relationships the most at risk. If we neglect ways to connect with and appreciate our best clients, we run the risk of letting the best parts of our business fall aside. Of course we need to solve problems, deal with difficult clients and look for new clients. But maintaining our relationships with our best clients is not only good for business, but it is good for our soul.

I like to surprise my best clients with gifts, notes of encouragement, and by singing their praises to others. I want my clients to know directly, and indirectly, how incredible they really are. It must never come from a place of manipulation or from an ulterior motive. It must come from a sincere place of love and gratitude. Intent matters.

If we can master never taking each other for granted, then we will have accomplished something great.

4) Don't be an asshole to others.

My dad was a man who was larger than life. But his outward persona didn't show the world who he really was.

My dad used to take me to work sometimes. He would park in an area that he wasn't allowed to park in and that puzzled me. He was a law-abiding man, so it just didn't make sense to me. Then he explained it to me one day.

I had noticed that whenever we walked into the building, he was always able to greet the security guards, custodians and secretaries by name and chat with them. I thought that was normal behavior. Apparently, it isn't. I have discovered that many people do not treat people who serve with respect and consideration. The fact that my father did that routinely, as well as purchasing nice gifts for them at Christmas, made him stand apart from everyone else. This was why he was allowed to park wherever the hell he wanted.

When we were walking around the building, he would frequently bump into someone he knew and would always engage them in a conversation that made them feel awesome about themselves. If there were small children with them, he would run to the store in the building and buy them chocolates as a treat. I was witness to these acts of kindness and just assumed that was how all adults behaved. What an incredible gift that was for me to be witness to.

What he taught me was to treat all people, regardless of status, with respect and humanity. In business, this can make the difference between mediocrity and success.

I know business owners who have strict policies that they can hide behind whenever there is a dispute with a client. But I also know business owners who know that those policies are merely a guideline and not law. I am the owner of my business and I know when to bend the rules. It is possible to do so in a way that respects my client and their needs, but also my own. If we can come out of a situation with both sides feeling heard and respected, then isn't that better than just winning by sticking to your policies?

We are seeing countless examples of this during the current pandemic. Some business owners are sticking to old policies and the backlash against them on social media has been dramatic. Airlines that refused to issue any refunds due to cancelled trips are just one example.

But those businesses that have bent the rules and allowed refunds, credits or bonuses for postponement of services have received only love. Their names will be remembered by their clients and they will be loyal customers for life.

Treating people with respect and consideration is not only the right thing to do, but it is also great for business.

5) Don't be an asshole to the truth.

I started this Chapter with a quote by Viktor Frankl from his book, Man's Search for Meaning, which is my favorite book of all time.

"When we are no longer able to change a situation, we are challenged to change ourselves.

Everything can be taken from a man but one thing: the last of the human freedoms—to choose one's attitude in any given set of circumstances, to choose one's own way.

Between stimulus and response there is a space. In that space is our power to choose our response. In our response lies our growth and our freedom."

I still have my father's tattered and annotated copy of this book. I have given dozens of copies away, and I've had many students read it as a part of an independent study project with me. It never gets old.

Too often life comes at us along the most unexpected avenues. We don't get to choose that. The choice comes in our response to it.

My mom's diagnosis of cancer was like that. Her death was like that. My father's death the day after my grandfather's funeral and a few weeks after his brother's death was like that.

We all have lists.

I read Man's Search For Meaning in one sitting when I was 18 years old. No one book has ever had such an impact on the way I have chosen to live my life. The truth is that we are not victims. There will be situations that we have no control over. There are times in our lives when we feel that we just cannot get a break. There are days that will feel hopeless.

But the truth is, we have a choice. We always have a choice in how to react to these. No one can make us react in a way of their choosing.

My father was an amazing dad, but he also happened to be an alcoholic. It was awful to watch him suffer, and to watch my mother and his dad, my grandfather who lived with us, suffer. I wish with all my heart that he hadn't had to go through all of it. I wish none of us did.

But there were some beautiful gifts that emerged from that experience. I learned to read people really well. My empathy is a fine-tuned instrument that I developed to protect me and my family, but which has become a gift that I am so grateful to have as a parent, partner, friend, teacher and business owner. I am not suggesting that I am glad my dad suffered, but I have found meaning in his and my suffering to make my life better.

I could have chosen to be suspicious, angry and hopeless. I did not. I chose instead trust, joy and hope.

My mother's diagnosis of cancer was one of the most painful experiences I have ever had. I was so infuriated that a woman who had suffered so much in her life, and had given so much good to this world, had to suffer this indignity. It was so unfair and I was angry. But once again, I had to choose. I chose instead to love her, and take the journey of her illness beside her. I did everything I could to make sure that she was able to do it on her own terms with dignity and love. I chose well.

The pandemic is forcing me to look at my business in a new light. Like everyone else, I get waves of panic while wondering if there will be any clients left when this is all done. It would be easy to allow circumstances to determine my response. But I have a choice. I choose to pause, reflect, pivot, and use this time to work on my business. It can be a tragedy or a gift. It is ultimately up to me to decide which it is.

"What matters, therefore, is not the meaning of life in general, but rather the specific meaning of a person's life at a given moment." -Viktor Frankl

Then a Pandemic Hits

Honestly, I do worry about what my business will look like coming out of this pandemic. Will I still be relevant? Will I be able to muster the drive and passion to start over?

I really am in the beginning part of my self-employed journey. I do have a chance to reinvent myself when this is over. But doing it differently? I am not sure. My focus and passion has always been to make a difference in the lives of people. My tool is the camera. The photographs are the evidence. I don't think that part will ever change.

I would do the following even more:

1) Fail even faster.

Running a business is inherently full of risks and lots of failures. The key to succeeding is to just fail as fast as you can so that you can experience the successes even faster. Perfection is not the goal. I thought I was already in that mindset, but I realize that analysis paralysis was a bigger barrier to my success than I thought at the time. You want to be thoughtful and deliberate, but you need to realize that analyzing something into perfection means that you will never have the opportunity to actually succeed. Good enough will often work. This is a tough pill for a perfectionist to swallow.

2) Ask for help.

I am stubborn. Stubborn as a mule. I think that I am smart enough to figure out things on my own, so I should. That has led to countless hours of diving in the weeds of my business, coming out no further ahead other than with a deep sense of frustration.

One good thing I did was invest in learning. I sought out information like it was a drug. I inhaled everything. I still do.

However, I have learned that sometimes the best thing I can do is hire someone or ask a friend for help. I have an incredible network of friends who are generous and kind. I hate imposing on people. I hate to ask. But I love to be asked. It occurred to me one day, what kind of asshole am I to deny others the joy of being asked? Should I not allow them the opportunity to share their expertise the way I like to? That realization shifted something in me, because you know, I am all about not being an asshole.

It is important not to use your friends. All relationships should always be in some kind of balance. Be willing to give to your friends in all kinds of ways. It can be with your knowledge, your encouragement, your inspiration or even gifts. Sometimes having an open heart and ears for your friends is the best gift you can give.

3) Trust.

I am a scientist by training. I believe in the testing of ideas, facts and the scientific method. However, a good scientist is also open to the possibility of new ideas.

I trust. It is who I am. There are so many things out of my control. There is a global pandemic. I am in a high-risk category. I trust the knowledge that I have will mitigate my risk of getting this virus. If I do get this virus, I trust in the statistics, the love of my family and friends, the incredible healthcare system in my country, and in my own determination that I will be one of the many that will recover from it. The rest is out of my hands.

I am just as scared as the next person. It requires continual effort to turn panic to caution, and to turn worry into love. But I do the work.

But what I really mean by trust, with regards to my business, is trusting that my message, my offerings, my passion for what I do, needs to be heard. It isn't about my ego, ultimately. What it really is, is about my stepping away from my ego and being there for others. I can no longer hide behind my own doubts and fears. I need to trust myself to step out of that and ultimately be there for others. It is not a selfish act to be heard. It is an act of love and service. That is something I wish I'd understood sooner.

.

About the Author

Anita Watkins is an award- winning professional photographer who specializes in portraits and personal branding. Her full-service approach guides her clients through the entire process of their shoot, starting with a consultation, which includes wardrobe, hair and makeup planning, then the shoot itself, and finally helping them select their favourite photos and choosing beautiful products all custom made in Italy.

Working out of her studio in London, Ontario, Canada, she has photographed hundreds of people and helped them rediscover themselves in the process. She has a gift of seeing people as they really are and revealing it in their portraits so that they see themselves the way the rest of the world sees them.

Starting her photography business after the age of 50 and hitting six figures in her first full-time year, she is the perfect example of someone that believes that it is okay to find your wings after you jump off the cliff.

She has achieved accreditation in the highly prestigious Sue Bryce's Portrait Masters program as well as Associate Photographer with Peter Hurley.

Connect with Anita:

www.facebook.com/anitawatkinsphotography
www.instagram.com/anitawatkinsphotography

CHAPTER FIVE

The "Sauce" That Brings it All Together

By Jennifer Matthews

Do you ever sit back and reflect on the personality traits that you have now, and wonder, "Did God give me these the day that I was born and have I grown into them, or were these personality traits that He's given me the opportunity to grow into as I've aged?"

It's an odd thought in itself, but so powerful when you look at decisions you've made (or have not been able to make) throughout your life, and how your personality has impacted those decisions.

When I sit back and think about who I was as a child, it's really hard for me to remember the type of person that I was. It's interesting, because it's only been in the last few years of personal development that I've been able to reflect on the type of child I was growing up and the types of conflicts that I got into. When speaking with people who knew me when I was a child, I can reflect back that WOW! I was given the initial stages of these gifts of my personality even when I was a child.

I've always known I'm assertive. I've always known I'm saucy. I'm smart and always interested in trying new things. At the very core of my being and my decisions, I know I am a warrior for people and for animals. However, it's only been through talking to people recently who knew me as a child that they have reminded me who I was as a child.

"I remember Jennifer was always funny."

"Jennifer was always there to help me if I got into trouble."

"Jennifer got in trouble for speaking out when something wasn't right."

I remembered even more through stories from my parents - I was that child who would bring baby mice home in a shoe box, if they had been left unattended by their parents. Those situations didn't always work out so well for the baby mice.

It's interesting to me when I reflect on my personality and my ability to accept who I am, who I am not, and those gifts that I was given and how they actually influence and impact how I lead my life.

Personality has played a huge role when I think about how I first got involved in business....it wasn't necessarily the traditional way. My dad owned his own business, and yet that didn't help me start my own business. In fact, he tried to talk me out of starting my own business.

For me, starting my own business came from a deep need I had in a very specific situation my husband and I were in at that time.

We had just had our first child and the thought of going back to work scared me.

"I am supposed to leave my child with a stranger? Or worse yet, family, who think they can do whatever they want with her? Have her eat mashed potatoes and nothing else for lunch? No naps? Switch her over to whole milk? Candy?"

No way! Not happening!

I didn't want anyone else raising my child. I wanted to be there every day. And even more importantly, my husband wanted the same thing for us. I had a great job and worked with the Provincial Government at the time. Great pension, great pay and benefits, and yet I did not want to leave my baby for any of that.

We tried to start a business, but as any entrepreneur should tell you, if you leave it too late, you're out of luck. And that's what happened. I had to go back to work. It broke my heart and worse still it broke my husband's heart, too. How could we have let this happen? Why were we so foolish that we did not prepare earlier? How did we not know better at the time?

While it was the worst thing for us at the time, it was the best thing that ever happened in the long run because it solidified for us that we would never put ourselves in the same position again. Ever.

Watching our tiny, 1-year old daughter sob and reach for us at daycare drop-offs was THE WORST feeling in the world. My husband told me that he sat in the car and cried afterwards, every day, was incredible fuel for our fires of determination.

We made a promise to each other that when I got pregnant again, we would be better dedicated to living the life we knew God wanted us to live.

Then the opportunity actually came around again and I was terrified! I was scared to take the jump of quitting my secure job. I was completely unsure if I had what it took to make a business work and earn real money from it.

I had the chance to buy an area-based license for Salsa Babies – a family dance/fitness company.

It was going to cost a lot of money! I was leaving a great job and benefits for the unknown.

I had no idea if I had the ability to make this work....

Then, like all God-given inspirations, I had a chat with my sister–in-law who reminded me of all the signs that had pointed me in this direction. She reminded me that God had put all of this in front of us for a purpose, and that this was something that I should be doing. It wasn't an easy decision, and thankfully my husband also had a great job so that made it a bit easier.

So I jumped!

I guess that piece of my personality has always been there, because as a child, I rarely took a moment to think about the consequences before jumping into situations. I am thankful for this personality trait today.

I had to borrow money from my parents, which was an awful thing to do because we were raised to borrow from no one, ever. I had to work hard to prove that I was worth the risk. I had to prove to myself that I could do it, but more importantly I had to prove to my dad that I wasn't going to squander this opportunity.

During the first 8 years of business, I developed a fantastic, strong following of moms and families who loved me and what I was doing in our community. Thirteen years later, those same moms are still cheering me on!

In 2013, an even scarier opportunity came to us. We had the opportunity to buy the entire Salsa Babies company. I knew it could be bigger and better. Being a licensee already, I could see where I wasn't being fully supported and I knew I would be able to improve the process and grow the company into what it should be.

There was that jump-before-you-think optimism again!

They say time and situation will present themselves, and that definitely happened here.

I knew at the time that the company was lacking a safety component and proper structure.

None of our team of instructors was teaching the same program – we all taught what we wanted, and called it Salsa Babies. There was no help available to us from the owner if we need to brainstorm or ran into trouble. Calls went unanswered. I knew there was SO much missing from this company and I knew I was the one who was being given the gift to make it happen.

As I purchased the company, I spoke to the former owner about the concerns I'd had. She dismissed every one of my considerations as being frivolous or ridiculous. I knew in that moment that I was absolutely the right one to take over this business.

I knew for this company to thrive and grow we needed to change the attitudes towards the safety and consistency of the classes. I knew there was a huge disconnect among the team. For people who worked solely from their homes but were part of a bigger group, this was a huge issue. I understood all of this, having grinded it out myself for years. I knew what moms really wanted.

I also understood that the biggest missing component was that our licensees/instructors needed the support of a team, and these people were coming to this business yet didn't know the first thing about how to start or run a business. I knew this company could be better and I knew I could do this and build it into what it should be.

Sounds fantastic and wonderful, right? I haven't shared with you what it cost me to make my dream and vision happen.

In order to buy this company, I needed to come up with $25, 000. I didn't know this at the time, but I was also being ripped off. I was told I was buying a company that had assets and made money every single month, when in reality I was buying a name, great branding, some original songs, some children's maracas, 5 instructors and a dream. Funny how, even with diligent research, once the paperwork is signed, the truth comes out. AND then you are given a choice – should I sue to get my money back for being misled, or do I eat the mistake, learn from it and move on?

That wasn't even the hardest part of this purchase for me.

I had to ask my dad for a loan to buy this company. So I prepared my pitch, got together all my numbers, had my business plan in hand and I was certain he would support me.

He said no.

He said he didn't believe that it was a legitimate business. He didn't believe that it was anything more than a fun hobby. And rightly so, for him - his own business was bricks and mortar, while mine was an online company. I was growing a business in a different time than he had done, and he couldn't understand it.

I was heartbroken that he didn't believe in me. I was determined to prove him wrong, and I fought many internal demons at the time who were also telling me I couldn't do it and that I wasn't enough to make this thing fly.

I came up against myself with this decision when I bought the company. I shit-talked myself a lot. I am a larger-sized woman who had no Latin dance background, and I had little experience running a business let alone a company - especially one which we wanted to take international.

Who was I to think that I could be the one to run this kind of company?

We hired a marketing consultant to help us figure out how we were going to take this company and rebuild it all, relaunch it all, and grow it. One of the first things my husband said during this process was, "Jennifer, you are absolutely the face of this company. You are a real mom, a real woman, and you are what people want to see in this company." His words made my skin crawl.

Have you ever had someone tell you something so raw and so truthful that it made you ill? And yet, he was right!

It took me a long time to think through what I, being the face of the company, looked like, because I was going to have to get raw with people, get honest with people and put myself out there. That went against every part of my being.

And then a conversation changed everything for me. A woman called our office wanting to speak with me about licensing. She changed everything. She said to me very directly, "Jennifer, I've been watching your company videos and I see two different Jennifers. One must be the old owner and one must be you. I want to know from you before I decide to purchase - which one is Jennifer Matthews?" That question made my entire body shake with fear. I thought I was going to throw up. Here it comes! Here is exactly what I was thinking was going to happen. She was going to judge me because I'm big, because I'm a white girl with no Latin American background. Who was I to be running this company? This woman was Columbian, so that made me even more apprehensive. The moment was coming. I knew this was going to happen. She was going to judge me, and I wasn't enough... I said to her, "I'm the one with curly hair, not the long straight hair, I'm the bigger one," and she said to me, "Perfect, I'm ready to buy."

She explained to me afterwards that the other Jennifer she had seen on the video did not look like an average mom - she looked out of touch and unreachable. She was not interested in being a part of a company run by that Jennifer. She reminded me of everything I knew and everything I promised myself I would make this company. Her answer and her faith in me gave me the fuel to step out and be my true self. We've had fantastic results while building my team and bringing families together. As I build this team of women who are licensees, and growing our company internationally, I've been clear to ensure that we bring on the right type of people. It's led to fantastic results and the Salsa Family team that I dreamed about building.

But something was still missing for me. Watching my business coach, John Michael Morgan, I knew I was missing a piece of me in this business. I thought back to when my sister-in-law was encouraging me and reminding me and showing me the signs that God had put into place for me, and I knew that there was a bigger piece missing.

I was trusted with this opportunity to assist women and help them grow a business to be able to support their families and raise their kids, just like I wanted. But if I'm honest, my faith was missing from all of this. This isn't about religious recruitment; it's about being grateful for what He gave me - my morals, my attributes, my beliefs and this opportunity. This came from Him.

I watched my coach John in awe. He was grateful and graceful in his business and he let people understand that his opportunity came from a higher place. I decided I wanted to do that for myself. So, I decided to dig in deeper and I was nervous. This was just like when I had been worried that people would judge me because I am large, or because I don't have a Latin background - would people be judging me because of my faith?

Would my team reject me if I came out and told them about my faith?

Would my team want to leave if I became a lot more honest when talking about who helped me lead this company?

As it turned out, absolutely not!

Women are drawn to me now even more so because of my honesty, because of my trustworthiness, and because of my generous and human warrior natures. Those gifts were given to me by a higher power and being honest about that has only helped me be a better person in business.

It is my absolute pleasure to embrace and propel this gift God has given me - and that is to lead and build up women in business with opportunities, growth, and support. You'd think that everything was fantastic after that. Ha! Business didn't get easier. In 2018, we decided to purchase two businesses that would support and grow our training program within Salsa Babies Limited.

The two main aspects of what we do are fitness-based and baby carrier-based. (A baby carrier is a tool used by families to carry their babies on their bodies hands-free.) We purchased a pre/post- natal fitness certification company as well as the only recognized babywearing education company in Canada. And as in all business acquisitions, there were always bumps along the way.

The first mistake I made with the purchase of the babywearing education company was not trusting my gut instinct. I doubted my feelings with this purchase, and I knew things would not end well with this company. I knew that the company's existing following, which the previous owner had grown, was very attached to her personally, and I also knew her following was not a market that would be attracted to our business. This group did not care about running a business with training; they only cared about helping. I knew there was nothing wrong with that, but that wasn't us as a company or where we wanted to take this company. The industry itself was and is a very volunteer-driven, inexperienced, hobbyist market.

What was I thinking??

Even with my 12+ years of business experience in this industry, I ignored my gut. My gut was telling me to slow down, and revamp what we were going to do. My gut was telling me not to offer the training and education in the same way, and to target a different audience. Yet the previous owner of the company promised and advised that this would go without a hitch, "Don't worry, people will be super supportive of what we're doing!"

As I got deeper into the purchase, I realized just how big of a mistake I had made. We paid to send different people to the previous owner's trainings all over Ontario, only to realize they each came back with a different set of information. There was no consistency with how the program was being run. There wasn't even a curriculum! The previous owner ran each training session differently and taught different ideas and topics at each training session. None of her following of people had the same training or information! She had been training people all over Canada and was speaking on this on an international level, yet with completely different information for all. She came to defend this to us afterwards by saying that she "wasn't a businessperson".

Nonetheless, my fighting spirit took over. I knew I had the knowledge, skills and outside professional resources to help not only this business, but also the industry itself (which is a hot-mess!). We had been in this industry for many years longer than the previous owner of the company had been. We knew what the program should look like and where it could go with right direction. There were a lot of changes needed.

We decided to jump in and do what we did best - we took this training program and our knowledge and skills, as well as consulting with industry professionals, and we completely rebuilt the training program. The whole time we paid the previous owner to consult with us on this and she stuck to her guns: "This is going to be great and they are going to love it!"

And then it completely blew up in our faces.

When we launched the new training, I got to watch it all implode in front of me. Because of the hobbyist nature of her audience before, who were followers and lovers of the program, I was accused of being nothing but a "corporate bitch". They accused me of being solely concerned with profits. They accused me of trying to profit off needy people because we were charging for professional training. Worse still, the previous owner of the company sat back silently and watched. She didn't speak up and tell them that this was the plan that she had approved. She let them believe that I had taken the company from her, when in reality we had purchased it from her. She didn't tell them that she had been paid to consult on this entire re-build and had approved every-thing along the way.

She let the fire build and it blew up.

The five trainers I had hired to offer these programs on a national level had to be let go, and it was my fault. I didn't trust my gut and I knew better. It's interesting, because having gone through this with Salsa Babies Ltd - buying a company that needed to be completely re-built - I should have known better and trusted myself. I knew that what was being promised to me was not the truth. So just like with Salsa Babies, we took down the company, we closed its doors temporarily, and we are currently doing a rebrand so we can continue to offer a better-quality program training and class to the right market this time.

This situation and the personal, untrue accusations about me almost gave me an ulcer. I felt ill for weeks af-terwards. Those closest to me who saw what happened and wanted to jump in and defend me (I said no, be-cause that would add fuel to my accusers' fires) asked me afterwards why I let them speak to me like that and why I didn't call out the former owner. I had video proof of all of our conversations. I had enough proof to throw her under the bus in a major way, and yet I stayed silent.

Why? Because this owner had just started a new job and this information, should I have put it out there, would put her job at risk. She was a single mom with 3 teenage boys. It was not my place to take her ability to feed her family away from her. So much for me being a heartless, corporate, profit-driven bitch.

I knew how to turn this around and not entirely lose my investment. I had done it before with Salsa Babies. I remembered a story one of my new licensees had shared with me, and it solidified my purpose when she said, "I looked at purchasing a Salsa Babies license many years ago before you owned the company and when I talked to the previous owner about her company, I left very dismayed. This wasn't a real company or a real opportunity. There was so much lacking from the company, from the program and from a training and safety standards perspective. I came across Salsa Babies again a few years later and took a chance to look at this again. The company looked very different and I didn't understand why. Now years later, with your guidance, this is an entirely different company. There's consistency everywhere, and on all platforms when I see the classes. There's been a huge influx of safety standards. It's just a completely different company. When I looked at the change of ownership, Jennifer, that's why I decided to invest."

I knew how to do all of these things and yet I let other people talk me out of it.

Getting comfortable in your skin, with who you are, with your personality gifts, is something that only comes as we age and grow. Being comfortable with who I am in business has also been a big piece of the conversation for me. I am not at all a fan of the terms "mompreneur", "fempreneur", or even "women in business". I feel those titles and labels do a disservice to women and in many instances, they discredit the professional nature of what we're trying to accomplish in business.

Men don't refer to themselves in this manner, so why do we need to? It doesn't help us. We are not held back because we are women. We are held back because of our beliefs in ourselves.

When have you ever heard a man say, "I am successful in business, because I am a man!" My vagina does not help me make the right decisions with the right people, nor does it hold me back. I dislike the terminology. I understand that many women relate to the terms and are drawn to them because they provide a community and a safe place to help businesses grow, but it's not my thing. In my experience there are far superior ways we can all help each other grow in business and relate to each other that have nothing to do with gender.

This belief in itself is a challenge, because my honesty turns some people off. Lots of people relate to these terms and that's great, but it's not for me. In wanting to be a champion to help women successfully run and grow businesses, I've had to build my armor, piece by piece, to fight for women with God leading me through this.

We've had to push through generalizations and assumptions about women and moms who run businesses. Again, that's why those terms frustrate me, because they don't help women build professional businesses for themselves!

How does one balance being a warrior for the human race and a champion for women in business with a deep-rooted desire to "just be a mom"? In the beginning, I needed an opportunity that provided flexibility so I could take my son to specialist appointments and go on class trips with my daughters. I needed to get my kids ready for their futures.

Now, how does one balance all that and be a beast of a leader when her life partner, her rock, her husband, gets sick? What does a warrior for the human race do when her rock suddenly is no longer able to be a rock? Two years after buying our biggest business opportunity, my husband got into a very sickening cycle with depression and ADHD. He struggled so badly and tested so high he should have been hospitalized. He couldn't work and he had no income for a year. We were one week away from our mortgage payment bouncing when we were given The Gift.

He never left our family's side. In that moment, God shifted his work to my husband. He helped my husband get to the doctor, and helped him start his two-year long journey back to health.

It was during this time that I was the most thankful for my business, my amazing Salsa Babies family and the flexibility we had. This, as it turned out, was THE hardest 2 years of my entire life - having to continue to live, continue to solo-parent and try and balance everything.

Struggle comes in the strangest forms. Like a metamorphosis, you must get very uncomfortable with struggles and change. In order to fly into your new life on the other side, you can't get there without discomfort. For my husband's metamorphosis, he was shown that God's gift to him is now a life of helping men and business owners who are struggling with depression and mental illness, to help them see what is on the other side. There are men struggling all around us, all around you, and they are silent. Now that we are on the other side, it is beautiful for me to be able to watch him use his own dark time to help other men.

For me, my gift is a new skill that I wasn't given as a child, but one that I needed to develop.

My personality traits, when I look back, have been pivotal to me becoming the business owner I am today. They have helped me while growing as a business owner, and through periods of struggle. Resiliency is now a skill I can take with me through the rest of my life.

When you look back on yourself as a child, what do the personality traits of that child offer you to help you walk through this life? How are you going to grow those traits and gifts? Are you going to stay true to that child and the innocence of not understanding those gifts in difficult moments? And what skills and gifts will you choose to collect along the way, to help that child step into the world to be a warrior for the human race?

Are you ready to soar with that child and those gifts?

Then a Pandemic Hits

The pandemic has caused so many business owners to question their suitability and sustainability to the long-term survival of their business. We are seeing business-es close down all around us - those owners are choosing to move on to their next paths. Maybe it was inevitable for them?

We are seeing businesses shift into new models of ser-vice - those owners are learning and shifting on the fly. The good ones are listening to their customers and giv-ing their customers what they are asking for. While I have not questioned my suitability or sustainability for my business, I have questioned some important pieces of my business that I had previously overlooked.

 The first main thing I overlooked with my business was having a solid financial system of savings. I WISH I had read Profit First by Mike Michalowicz as I was starting our corporation. It would have made the difference be-tween me currently "getting battered by the storm" and me wanting to "ride out the storm".

There is always time to start, though, and I have consist-ently been a quick implementer. Even during the pan-demic, I have been able to make my business stronger financially.

The second thing I overlooked was ensuring our licens-ing contracts didn't leave us without income. I have lost licensees during the pandemic, due to the stress and unknowns of the pandemic. I didn't anticipate the loss, though, because I learned early on the significance of building a close-knit and connected team, and that is how we drive the business. I had assumed that if I built a tight ship they would all stay, no matter how rough the waves were.

What I have learned is that without proper protections in place, it doesn't matter how tight your team is; in times of panic, if they are not required to stay on board and ride out the storm, they will jump ship. It comes down to a simple mistake we made. We allowed our licensees to terminate their contracts for any reason at any time, without financial repercussions for breaking their contract early.

I have paid a steep price for that financially, and despite being close to all of these women, they left anyway without a thought to the overall well-being of the company and the team of women left behind. This has been painful, but we learned from it and we will evolve to ensure our WHOLE team has what they need to feel protected and supported in business with us in the future.

About the Author

Jennifer Matthews is best described as a passionate woman. As a mother of 3, a wife, animal lover and the owner of multiple businesses with team members around the world, her faith is a leading driver in all of those roles.

Her unique ability to lead, teach and empower women by using information gathering and sensing their energies, helps her to be an enthusiastic and magnetic leader in her field and helping the women she supports to grow personally and professionally.

Her main business, Salsa Babies Ltd, has grown under her leadership, from being closed down in 2013 (when she purchased the company), to now offering 6 distinct programs to families in eleven countries around the world.

Connect with Jennifer: www.salsababies.com

CHAPTER SIX

The Spectacular in an Unspectacular Life – Lessons from Len

by Rhett Hawkins

Who the heck is Len? And why do I call my dad, Len? I was recently asked that very question, as I believe people think it is a sign of disrespect. I think it came about when we were younger and dad (Len) was our coach. He'd tell everyone on the team, "Don't call me Mr. Hawkins. My name is Len, so call me Coach Len." I think that is where it came from and just shows how Len was one to make people feel comfortable, and encourage them not to think of him as a person with power over them. One of the hardest things to do in life is to influence without power. I'd argue it's pretty much impossible in business to do so. Hierarchy seems to reign supreme, whatever line of work you are in. However, Len would bring things down to the same level for all, whether it was a youth sports team or a boardroom. You'd soon learn that he knew what he was talking about and would listen attentively. That's true leadership.

This chapter will touch on more of the lessons I have learned in hopes of teaching and inspiring you as they have me. One chapter will never cover them all; maybe we'll save some for the follow up to this book.

Who is Rhett Hawkins?

So, who the heck is Rhett Hawkins? As the title of the chapter indicates, I really think I'm nobody particularly special. I've done nothing extraordinary, I haven't gone through any life-altering struggles that are beyond the norm, nor have I conquered any enemies that threaten our freedoms. Rhett Hawkins is an average guy, living an average life. I grew up on our family's cash crop and beef farm in the 70's and 80's. When I was young, I really didn't enjoy working on the farm, but as I grew older I loved that we grew up learning that work ethic. We moved off the farm when I was 16, when our father's company was sold and we had to move closer to his office. I struggled in school for a while, trying to meet new people and fit into a new school. In grade 12, things started to click academically, and I did well enough throughout the remainder of high school to get into university. I was focused on business and marketing, but also enjoyed psychology as it gave me an insight into how people think. After university I got a job at Grey Advertising and worked as a media coordinator, then a planner for Warner Brother Movies. Big job, right? That job taught me that I wanted to somehow work back in agriculture. The people are real in agriculture, and I wanted more of that back in my life. I took a job at a mid-sized advertising agency that was focused on "life sciences", Agriculture was one of those "life sciences," and I've remained in the agricultural industry ever since - working, owning, planning, and managing campaigns, people and teams at the client, agency, and now media side of the business. I've had opportunities to make more money, have bigger jobs, and have what some might deem a more successful career. And this is where I bring it back full circle, and now the story at the beginning of the chapter will make more sense. Along the way, my wife, Jennifer, and I had two children - Kaeden and Delphine. My priorities were really rocked once they came into the picture. I didn't have a farm to help teach them the ways of the world, but I could choose a career that kept me around them more than not. That was where the decision to choose a spectacularly unspectacular life came from. I know it's an oxymoron, but I think readers will appreciate the normalcy in the wording.

In talking through the opportunity to write a chapter for this book, the idea was about being average and telling a story around that seemed to be something that we felt the reader may be interested in. For years, we've all heard of extraordinary feats from celebrity authors and speakers. And what have we learned? Their efforts and their accomplishments impress us, yes. Then what happens? At some point, we learn that they don't share our core values. Simply, we learn that they were not good people. They let us down. Who cares how much money you have, or about your celebrity or your big house and speaking tour if you've got no soul? My chapter is about all of us having permission to live extraordinary lives in ordinary ways.

Let's get back to working hard, doing the right thing, and prioritizing the right things in life. Let's get back to core values that help drive our version of success. In our family, we refer to those core values as "Lessons from Len". I learned many lessons from my dad and hope to share a few of those with you here.

Who is Len Hawkins?

When I originally sat down to write about the lessons that my dad had taught me, I meant to write an entire book and still do, but I was both inspired and demotivated after reading, "Nine Lessons I learned from my Father", by Murray Howe. A majority of the lessons Murray shared about his dad, Gordie Howe, could have been written about my own father. The only thing going through my head was, "Why would anyone care about these lessons from Len Hawkins when they can read about Gordie Howe?"

I've spent a good amount of time over the past couple of years thinking about who would care and why it matters. In the end, I have concluded that the "who" cares doesn't really matter. What matters most is that there were lessons, whether overt or not, and those who spent time around our father remember them. It's not like Len wrote these lessons down. He never referred to lessons of any sort. He just went about his life in a manner that we noticed, respected, and tried to emulate.

Before we get into some of the lessons, I think it's important to have a little perspective about Len's upbringing. His past obviously helped define him and make him into a person worth writing about. Leonard William Hawkins was born February 23, 1942, in London, Ontario. He had a twin, but his brother was stillborn. He was born to Marjorie and Clarence Hawkins, who were farmers. Len worked on the farm, went to school in a one-room schoolhouse, and was raised like many farm kids of the era. He excelled at school and was a decent hockey player. His parents were simple people of simple means. Both his parents liked to have a good time and often had music playing at home. Len loved the farm, but aspired to learn more about the world. His parents didn't encourage his education or think it was required, but Len went to university nonetheless. During that time his parents got divorced, which was taboo in the 60s. Many have a more challenging upbringing, but one has to wonder how these events helped shape the person Len would become.

Len went onto a fairly successful career in sales and business with various agricultural companies. He ended his career working with one of these companies in China, where he and my mom lived for 4 years. From simple beginnings on an Anderson Corners farm in Southwestern Ontario, and from Canada to Beijing, China.

I think the main lesson from Len would be summed up by the famous Maya Angelou quote; "I've learned that people will forget what you said, people will forget what you did, but people will never forget how you made them feel."

I've watched Len with thousands of people; he always asked them about what they were doing, where they had been, and he took a genuine interest in them. I know it's not just idle chatter, as I'll hear him share details from these conversations with others. He remembers people because he cares about people. People feel that, which has to be why Len has so many friends, acquaintances, and raving fans around the world.

I hope to inspire you with some of the lessons Len has taught me over the years. Len didn't just teach my siblings and I these lessons. I think it's another lesson to always "share" your knowledge. Some people think knowledge is power, and try to bully people and leverage situations with that knowledge. However, we are in different times where anybody can just get on Google and find out fact or fiction about most things. Social media shares our lives, warts and all, by the second. There is nowhere to hide anymore. This chapter isn't about whether I think those things are good or bad; they are what they are. Getting back to the idea of sharing, Len always shares what he knows and goes out of his way to help mentor those he has worked with and become friends with in life. I wanted to share a few of those experiences from others that Len has helped over the years:

100% Effort

There's no sense doing something if you don't give it your all. This lesson rings in my ears daily as I raise my kids. Remember, I didn't do anything spectacular in life, but I'd like to think I got a lot out of what I was given. I've done well at most things that I've put 100% effort into. Len always said that if you put the effort in, you will be rewarded. And he was right. Sometimes, you fall back - A LOT – but, in the end, effort prevails. It's tough to see that when you're young, but it is a recipe for success in anything you do in life.

An example of this is from early in my career when I was working at a Marketing Communication Company. There were two of us who would be there until all hours of the night or morning. We'd be the first two there in the morning as well. A lot of people told me that it wasn't worth it. The company wasn't paying me more for the effort, so why do it? At the time, I could only answer that it would pay off in the long run. Did it pay off with money? Not in the short-term, but likely in the long-term. What it did was give me a masterclass in business and running a company. I was there to see what other managers were doing and how they managed the business. I didn't just see all the good stuff either. You see the bad stuff too when you're there that late at night. I was putting in 80-100 hours a week when I first started my career. I wouldn't change that for anything. This was pre-kids, so it was the perfect opportunity to put that time in and learn. It was all about the learning curve and getting me to the top of it as quick as possible. There were plenty of people smarter than I was, but in the end, few put the time in. I have carried that recipe with me for a long time. Once the kids came, I had what I had learned and can make decisions much more quickly. What used to take me until 2am in the morning might take me 10 minutes now. That is what the effort has afforded me.

I see people my age and older struggle with decision-making or coming up with solutions. They get paralyzed when things go wrong and can't function. In the end, 100% effort pays off. In my case, it's paid off with extra time to spend with my kids. That may consist of driving them around the country to their sports events, but at least I'm able to spend that time with them now. Those car rides can be special.

Know Where Home Is

As I write this section, I am on my way to our University of Guelph annual boys' trip. We used to play in an annual hockey tournament, but found we were all getting a little long in the tooth to keep trying to compete. Len and all his children went to Guelph, so it is a source of pride for all of us. Before the trips he'd always have a subtle way of reminding me the value of these friends and any truly great friends. He's asked me on a few occasions where I considered "home" to be. We've moved around a lot, which many do. After I give my answer, he always reminds me of the story of his friends who have moved around a lot. He always knew where his "center" was and when he retired, he settled in St. Mary's, Ontario. It's where he was raised and where a majority of his friends lived, and was at least close to a number of them. In his anecdote, he said he had always been surprised and sad at how many of his friends and colleagues upon retirement did not know where they considered home to be. They'd lost touch with friends and family and no longer had a place they considered home. This annual boys' trip is something I make every effort to attend. I think I've only missed two; one early in my career when priorities were out of whack, and another when my son got sick. One of those was a good reason to miss it for. The boys are my compass, and always remind me where home is. Len is right. Knowing where home is is another way of making sure you stay in touch with friends, know what is important in life, and have your priorities in check.

It's Not About "Stuff"

I was at dinner with friends of our family recently. I say "family" as I met these people through Len. They have now become friends of all of us. Another character trait of Len's has been his desire and ability to connect people. If he considers someone a friend, he likes to connect those people to others. Who has too many friends, right? That's a whole other story in itself. We started talking about clothes and how Len always wore simple things. It reminded me that he never really spent any money on himself. He didn't grow up with a lot of money, and learned how to stretch a dollar early on in life. Recently, he decided to give one pair of his old skates to our family. These skates are the ones that you see artists do paintings of. Old, leather, tube skates that have seen more ice than the Arctic Circle. Len told the story behind them. Below is that letter:

The Story Behind These Skates

*During my minor hockey days, my parents could only af-
ford 2nd hand skates. However, when I started playing
Junior B hockey for the [St. Mary's] Lincolns and had
some of my own money, I decided to purchase a good pair
of skates.*

*In 1961, a new pair of Bauer skates would run $100,
which was way out of my price range. Lucky for me, there
was a player on my team who had worn these skates for a
couple of months and grown out of them. I was able to
buy these relatively new skates for $50 – half price!*

*I played one year of Jr B, four years of Redmen [Universi-
ty of Guelph's team at the time], three years of Old Tim-
ers, and coached for over 15 years – with the same pair of
skates. The boots and blades are still in decent condition,
but the rivets holding them together have long needed re-
placing.*

*It just proves that they don't make skates to last as long
as they once did.*

He's right that "they don't make them like they used to",
but this is also an example of his dislike of extravagance,
his love of a bargain, and his respect for durability. If it
works, it's still useful. Those skates are a reminder to be
frugal, humble, and again, put your time and effort into
the things that matter. The skates don't matter. The en-
gagement with us as a coach mattered for him. Long

after his coaching days, he'd go out with his grandchildren on those skates. They'd laugh at how old they were, of course. But that was all part of it – while entertaining, he was always teaching us that the "things" don't matter. Playing a game where you learned life lessons and made life-long friendships mattered. The blades will be part of our décor for the rest of our lives and likely for many generations to come. They will remind us daily to be mindful of the material things in life. An old pair of skates does the same thing as a new pair, but with so much more meaning.

It's About Singles, Not Home Runs

This idea may not be popular with where Major League Baseball has gone the past few years. In life and in baseball, the long ball is the sizzle. It's spectacular, it gets everyone excited, and it gets you quick ascent in the game of life. Many people looking for the quick win are still looking. If you don't put the time in to do the little things right, you don't set yourself up to ever get around those bases. The idea is to set up the infrastructure of your life.

Like a city, roads need to be built, bridges constructed, power lines raised, and water towers developed. Len has always maintained great relationships with people. He is there when they need him and calls upon people when he needs them. He keeps things simple, but that simplicity when building those blocks of life has paid off with a life and career with meaning. He has friends across the globe and experiences to last many lifetimes.

One example of this is when Len worked in China for Delta and Pineland. Think about being in your late 50's and moving from Canada to China. We were all out of the house – at university or in the workforce. There was nothing holding our parents back but the fear of the unknown. Len took us out for drinks one evening and told us about the opportunity. Our collective comment was, "What would you tell us to do?" Not long after, the decision was made – our parents would be moving to China for four years. We all visited them while they were there. We were introduced to many of the people Len worked with and took part in our fair share of banquets. Not unexpectedly, Len seemed to have created relationships and gained respect with people across the globe. There was one person in particular that Len took under his wing. Kathleen Wong was a young, educated, professional working at DP&L. Here is what she had to say about meeting and working with Len:

> *The time I worked with Len was just after I left an accounting firm. The workload with the accounting firm was extremely taxing. The earliest time I could leave the office was 9pm. It was exhausting. When I started working for Len at DP&L, I was able to leave at 5:30pm. I was not well suited to this "rhythm", so I asked Len if I could create some projects to work on outside of the office. One day, in the corridor of an office building, Len asked me the question, "is life for work or is work for life?" I was shocked, honestly, I'd never thought about life or work this way. From that day forward, I tried to re-think about the purpose of my life and I still keep searching. It all started from that conversation in the corridor.*

Character translates no matter where you grow up. Bringing this back to baseball, Kathleen was missing out on life. She was trying to hit the home run to career stardom. She thought that hours meant worth and success. As Len reminded or taught her, do a good job every day. Go enjoy your life after work and recharge for the next day. That daily routine of doing your best, winning the day, then repeat will get you where you want to go. And as Mick Jagger sang, "You might find sometimes, you get what you need".

Own your Mistakes – Be Accountable

Without going into too much detail here, it is safe to say that Len (and his children) were and are not angels. We all got into our fair share of mischief in this life and would never be hypocritical in judging others' actions. However, we did learn early on that we had to own up to our mistakes and pay the consequences. Len would ensure our safety, but we had to own our actions. We would actually have family meetings if one of us got into serious trouble. Len would outline the issue, talk about why it was bad, have us talk about our thoughts to ensure we knew the "why" behind why it was bad, then talk about the repercussions. Sounds like a business, doesn't it? It also ensured there was nothing misunderstood. Everyone knew why I or any of us was in trouble, so they knew the real story. It also put the perpetrator on the spot – do you really want to go through that again? One particular time at an age too young, I had a cousin who bought my friends and I some beer. We'd planned to meet at a house for the exchange, but they were late and we needed to start walking to where we were meeting more friends. My cousin somehow found us (it was a small town, of course) while driving around the town. They quickly pulled over and threw us the beer in a knapsack. Unbeknownst to any of us, the homeowner of the driveway we were in was at their window during the exchange. They called the police and took down the license plate number. As we walked off with our beer – keep in mind, there were about 8 of us and a 12 pack, which reminds us how silly we were – I split off to meet a girl and escort her to a pre-dance party. I didn't get far before a police car pulled up. Of course, I had the knapsack and all my friends had dispersed. I was caught red-handed, as they say. I don't want to dwell on the details of the stupidity of my actions. It only provides the background to what became a Len-led family meeting and a one-year grounding. The other impressive thing is that I spent that whole year grounded – no early time off for good deeds. It was a long year. It was also a lifetime lesson. My parents didn't shy away from the bad act. It was an open book in our family and in the community. Len taught us all accountability and this was one of the bigger examples of how I learned that. I won't go into my siblings' stories – that's likely another book. However, we did have a cousin that was willing to tell her story. Sonja Fletcher is our first cousin on my dad's side. She and my sister, Laurie, are the same age and are friends as well as relatives. Here's her own story of accountability and life lessons from Len:

I spent many of my days at the Hawkins household as I am friends with Len's daughter, Laurie. I always felt very at home there....maybe sometimes too much! I remember Len being a busy guy...he farmed and was also on the road working a lot. When he was home, it was family time. With Len around, there was always laughing and good conversation. I always have loved that when I see Len, I get a big hug and he calls me "his favorite Fletcher girl!"

What is Len about? Len had a very successful career, and you can see that all of his children have followed in his footsteps. He is so proud of all of his family. Being around him, he always reminded all of us to work hard but have fun along the way. Be that leader...do not follow.

He taught us about respect and accountability. I remember very clearly a party happening when Len and Janice were away. There were some things that could not be cleaned up or fixed before they got back. One being the antique staircase spindles that somebody had broken. I remember Len having a very clear discussion with one of Steven's friends in his "office" at the house. He made him come over and meet with him. That young man was made accountable for what he had done. I am sure to this day he remembers that conversation with Len and for Len teaching him as well about respect.

Sonja was not the only one to witness or take part in being held accountable. You'll notice it was always a conversation. It was respectful, calm, and with understanding. Nobody was let off the hook, but they weren't bullied or physically harmed in any way. As I said earlier, it was a lot like a business meeting. Or at least how a good one should take place if there's a crucial conversation to be had. You see a lot of people today that can't have those conversations – on either side. I've worked with many a manager who would make HR have the conversations they couldn't have or they just wouldn't address the issue. I've also seen parents let their kids get away with things that won't help them later in life. Being grounded now means saying the words rather than actually being grounded. Do what you say you're going to do, and follow through. Be accountable for your actions and own up to them when you should. Pretty simple stuff in theory, but how often does society practice this anymore? Bring back the family meeting. You won't regret it.

Never Let Them See You Sweat

Len has an uncanny ability to perform under pressure. No matter the situation, he comes at it relaxed and calm. That calming approach calms everyone around him. Have you ever been involved in a situation where somebody is hurried and panicked? They start making everyone hurried and panicked and things never run as smoothly. What will be, will be. Calm down, think about it, and drive on. A lot of the time, people won't even know there's a problem if you don't act like there is. If they do know there's a problem, they'll respect your calmness and ability to act under pressure. This goes for your career and personal life. The opposite side of this is that if you ever have a reason to raise your voice and show anger, people will listen. If you're always 'on' people and sweating every detail, people will disengage and become desensitized to your rants. Save your rants for when they are truly needed and they will be more meaningful.

I also never heard my dad say that he'd had a hard day or was working too hard. Looking back, he was always working. He always had a notepad or was on the phone or in his office. His work-life balance was full integration of work and life. I assume that part of that is that he truly loved his work, so it never really felt like work. I have noticed in my career that those that are always complaining about how busy they are don't get a lot done. They are so busy talking about being busy that they leave little time for the work part. Then they panic, then make everyone else cover for them, and we're back to the first part of this section. Never letting them see you sweat means that you can handle it, take the time and plan to enable yourself to handle it, and then move on to the next task without a lot of fanfare.

An example my dad has shared with me that is relevant here is about the time he had to fire a sales rep who was working for him. This particular rep would tell Len that everything was great in the field; he was working very hard to keep up with customer needs, and developing good rapport with them. Len will tell you that it is important, no matter what level you're at, to stay connected with your customer (another lesson that we'll touch on later). With this in mind, Len decided to go on the road with his sales rep one day to visit their customers. It became increasingly apparent during the visits that the rep had not been visiting his customers. One can only assume what he was doing, but each customer said that they were not satisfied and that the rep was not calling on them. Beware of those who talk about how busy they are! They are over-compensating for their lack of work or competence.

Family First

We heard from Kathleen Wong earlier in this chapter. I think it's amazing that Len and Janice were able to form such a deep and meaningful relationship with a person while in China. Kathleen is their daughter from their time there. They have that type of connection that continues to this day. Len was an only child, from a large extended family. He keeps in contact with all of his relatives and is a catalyst to the reunions held every year. I'll be honest, I do a bad job of attending those. There always seems to be an excuse, as we all might have with young children and busy work lives. Len doesn't pester, though. He keeps us informed of the family in email and on the phone. He always lets us know the dates of the reunion and softly reminds us that it'd be good for us to attend. We will make it this year! Our nuclear family lives all over the world. My brother currently lives in Switzerland, my sister in Ontario, and I in Illinois. Technology makes it easier to keep in touch. WhatsApp has been a nice way to stay connected, but nothing can replace getting together in person. Len had a serious health scare a few years ago. We all rushed home and were pretty much ready to give him his last rights. Len's a farm boy from Anderson Corners, though, and proved his resilience once again. He pulled through and has made a remarkable recovery. We're blessed to have him with us and don't take that for granted. The other thing we didn't take for granted was that we need to be together more as a family. Since that day, we've all made more effort to see each other a couple of times a year. We all say that Len was teaching us another lesson – and went through hell to teach it to us. One of the lessons in this chapter is "Know where home is". An even greater lesson is to keep in touch with your family – nobody knows you like them – warts and all. It's pretty cool to have a sibling, cousin, and somebody that shares how you came to be in this world. Don't ever forget that. Len hasn't. Len also knows that family can go beyond bloodlines. You've heard a number of our stories from the family, but Kathleen's example below shows us how Len is family-oriented no matter where he is in the world. He knows his priorities, which keeps decisions simple when you have to choose:

I remember there was an important business meeting in Shanghai and Len originally planned to attend. Janice, his wife, had injured her knee. Len cancelled his trip because he needed to accompany Janice to get surgery in Beijing. He often talked family-first, but I didn't really believe that until he walked the talk.

Kathleen's example reminded me of another family-first example from Len. Long after he'd moved to China for the experience of a lifetime, I learned of a job offer he'd turned down early in his career. He was offered the chance to chase unicorns and climb the corporate ladder by moving to the US. It was a big job that would have set him up for future opportunity. He did not accept that job. Instead he stayed on the farm, where he felt he could best raise his three kids during their early years. I believe we all benefited from that decision. In the end, he was rewarded with another opportunity when he was ready – on his terms and at the right time.

Patience Pays Off

There are so many lessons that it was hard to just pick a few for this chapter. My goal has always been to write a book on all the lessons we and others have learned from my dad. This chapter can serve as a teaser to a future, longer version. There's really not a conversation that I have with my dad where I don't go, "Hey, there he goes again, that was a lesson hidden in subtlety". The lessons are now less overt than they might have been in our youth. He's built the bases, and now he just reinforces them from time to time. I often wonder if he is consciously teaching us on purpose. As with those that teach us the biggest lessons, I very much doubt it. I think he's just Len being Len, which having a front row seat for has been the very best experience a life can offer

About the Author

Rhett Hawkins is a lifelong advocate of agriculture, husband, father, son – and hopefully a friend to a few as well. His values were born out of being raised on a farm outside of a small town in Southern Ontario. Rhett's dad, Leonard Hawkins, brought him to a meeting at an advertising agency when Rhett was in Highschool. That experience led him down a path to understand more about branding, marketing, psychology, and how all that works in the construct of business. You could say Rhett is a curious person, who Amazon loves due to his book spend. He has worked in and out of Agriculture – being a partner in two Advertising Agencies, then parlaying that into the Client and Media side of the industry he serves. Rhett currently lives in the US with his wife, daughter, and son.

Connect with Rhett:

linkedin.com/in/rhetthawkins

CHAPTER SEVEN

Life is Not a Dress Rehearsal

By Kris Dureau

I took a huge chance with my life, and the lives of my family. I went from being a member of one of the most trusted professions as a fire fighter, to one of the least trusted professions; a financial advisor. I find that people often feel that investing isn't as transparent as it should be, and I fully agree with that. My job is and has been to help people, whether as a businessman or a firefighter.

I always had an interest in finance. Even as a child, I would try to figure out how I could make more income from working multiple jobs so that I could afford the things I wanted to buy. I used to get an allowance, but I wanted more than that, so I also had a paper route and worked at a gas station. I knew then that if I worked hard at my jobs, I'd make money, and if I could resist the temptation of instant gratification and save the money I earned, I could buy nicer things later on.

In my early twenties I was a fire fighter for fifteen years and a paramedic for six years. In my off-time I kept myself in great shape at the gym and competed in body building at a national level. From twenty-two years old until I was about thirty, I committed myself completely to those careers, and I made a good income doing them, so I was able to save quite a bit. I wanted to do as much as I could with the money I'd made, so I started learning about investments.

At the beginning, much of what I learned was through self-education. The more I learned, the more I wanted to know, so I started taking courses. It was so fascinating to me that I decided to get into finance, and the classes became a way to gradually launch myself into a new career.

With a wife at home, I wanted to be judicious about the time I used to study, and I was lucky that for fire fighters, there can be some downtime during some of the shifts. We weren't always going out on calls or doing emergency training every minute of the twenty-four hour shift. For years I did my education in my downtime while I was at the fire house as well as late nights at home, once my wife went to bed, so it wouldn't take away from my family time.

I earned my insurance and financial licenses, and then continued to go after other designations. I wanted to expand my skillset beyond the standard levels of a financial advisor. I started with a Certified Health Specialist (CHS) designation, followed by becoming a Certified Financial Planner (CFP). After that I became the second person in Canada to become a Certified Cash Flow Specialist (CCS). I am currently obtaining a designation as a Chartered Investment Manager (CIM).

Things were going fine and moving along. The more I learned, the more it seemed that others around me took a greater interest in what I was doing. My friends and family began coming to me with questions; such as handling cash flow, changing careers, or asking me how to invest or save. I was happy to help them. Guys and gals at the fire hall started asking me for advice as well, and my path to becoming a financial advisor really developed from there; in fact, it exploded.

Fire fighters, police officers, and paramedics all wanted help investing and making the right choices with their money and their futures, and there were a lot of them. Even the heads at the first finance company I worked for were surprised because I had so many clients right from the start. It was a nationwide company, and in my first few months working for them I made it into one of their top ten lists of advisors. Most people starting out in that kind of a career only work with their family and friends at the beginning. I had an enormous base of emergency service workers who were ready to become my clients. It was really good for them as well as for me, because I was interested in helping people with planning that wasn't attached to product, and they knew they could trust me.

Fire fighting in Canada is considered a revered job; people rarely leave that career, since it's so difficult to get into to begin with. Fire fighters are well respected, they make good money, and leaving is simply thought of as crazy and unconventional. I took a big chance to leave all of that to own my own business with no guarantees and benefits to support a family of five. Then, as happens to so many people, life threw my family and I a serious curve ball, and everything changed.

It was Father's Day weekend of 2017, and my family and I were going to go up to our cottage for the weekend. I was at my older daughter's soccer game when my wife called me. Our four year old daughter Brooklyn wasn't feeling well, and my wife had taken her to the hospital to be checked.

It was one of those phone calls you never want to get. With the most horrific tone in her voice, my wife told me that as she was walking into the hospital with our daughter, Brooklyn's body went completely limp in her arms; her eyes rolled back in her head, and she went unresponsive. At first she thought our baby had died in her arms, but then an emergency room doctor who happened to be coming off the night shift saw them, and told my wife to get to the front desk immediately and tell them that she had an unresponsive child, and he followed her.

When my wife called me, she had no idea yet what was happening. It was the darkest day of my entire life. I was thirty minutes away, but I got to the hospital as fast as I could with our older daughter and our son. I burst through the doors asking what was going on, and I was told that Brooklyn had Kawasaki disease; something very rare, and potentially life threatening if not treated early enough. I had never heard of this disease before, and the more the doctors informed us of, the more terrified I became.

There was a team of doctors consulting outside of my daughter's room. They let us know that the disease had begun to attack the arteries of her heart, and she needed a blood transfusion right away to save her life.

It took one thousand blood donors to make up the one bag of the plasma that was needed for the infusion. Luckily it worked. Her life had been saved, but there was permanent damage done to her heart, and she will have to be monitored for the rest of her life.

Going through that harrowing experience reset my entire perspective. I began thinking about what I was doing; working so many hours all the time, getting caught in the proverbial hamster wheel of trying to work hard and get ahead. That's a mindset that's ingrained in most of us as young people, and it stays with us throughout our lives. I was missing some of the best years of my life, laboring away for the future when the future is never guaranteed, and missing out so much on the present. I knew it was time to change the way I was living my life.

At that point I had been a financial advisor for a while, helping clients with investments and financial planning, and designing their retirements for later in life, but after going through my experience with Brooklyn, I realized I needed to shift my focus. I realized I should be helping my clients get the most out of their lives today, while still ensuring a strong future.

Life can change in a single moment, and I learned that personally with my experience with Brooklyn, even after seeing it happen to others. There were so many times when I responded to emergency calls for people who had woken up, put on their suit or uniform, and gone off to work, thinking they would have the rest of their lives, but then they never went back home.

I'd be in the back of the ambulance, or showing up for a medical call, and I'd see fear in a spouse's eyes for their significant other, knowing that the situation was really bad. Sometimes I'd sit the spouse beside me in the back of the ambulance while I was taking care of things, so they could talk to their loved one. I would hear them say, 'don't worry, we're still going to take that trip, or continue our plans'. They'd be talking and I'd be thinking, 'there's a very good chance that's not going to happen'.

Seeing that so many times, and then going through the experience with our daughter, made me take a different approach to helping people with their finances. I really push for my clients to live in the moment, while still planning for the future without focusing too much on tomorrow, because it's never promised. I think the reality of life and death isn't talked about enough. I often advise many of my retired clients to spend their money, and most of them haven't heard anything like that from a financial professional before.

I tell them, 'we've done all the planning, we've gone through numerous scenarios to show you are going to be ok, and if the money is there, it doesn't make sense if you don't use it to live right now'. They don't know when their time will be gone; none of us do. The point is to live as well as we can, while we can.

Understanding that concept has made one of the biggest differences in my life now, and it has become an inherent part of the lifestyle planning that I help others with. During my time as a fire fighter, I'd respond to people who woke up thinking it was a day like any other day, but their lives either ended, or were seriously altered from that point.

When I help people now, I focus heavily on where they are in their lives presently, and I ask them why they're in front of me. Sometimes they'll say for retirement, or to increase their wealth, but that's not the answer. We look at the real reasons behind their desire for more money, and I teach them that wealth is a tool to enhance their lives, but the main objective of their lives isn't to achieve more wealth.

I spend time showing them a return on where they are in life right now. Most people know what the return on their investments is. They can look that up and see the numbers; see the return, but we use different tools to show them where they are in their current life stage. We talk about their health, relationships, work, well-being, and security, among several other important factors.

For a lot of people, it's the first time they've ever seen a score on their life. I tell them that there's no correct answer; everyone places differently. It's illuminated on the screen and they can see for themselves what that value is.

Some scores are higher than others. A high score in a particular field indicates contentment or happiness with it, while a low score shows that there are situations that need to be addressed. We look at which ones are low, and which are high, and why they're that way, and then we ask questions about how we can improve those areas where the scores are lower, while keeping the higher scores where they are.

It quantifies a life discussion, but more importantly, it gives us a baseline to start from. For example, it may be great that the person's net worth goes up every year, which is a component of the whole and that's something that most financial advisors focus on, but it makes a lot more sense to make sure that the return on their current life stage and where they're at is going up as well as their net worth.

If a client is just focusing on their net worth but there are other negative factors like they hate their work, or they don't like the area that they live in, or perhaps they're stressed because of those things, and they feel that there are other factors in their lives that are affecting them in a negative way; those are things that must be changed to give them a better return on their life. Any number of situations might be out of line with the client's goals; maybe like most people, they aren't where they thought they'd be at that point in their lives, or perhaps they don't have relationships with parents or family members that they should, and because of the stress of it all, their health isn't what it should be. All of that is much more important than whether or not they have a good mutual fund.

I worked with one couple who thought they were five years from retirement. They'd never had a proper plan done, and everything they did have, they'd done on their own. We spent some time going over where they were in life, and looked at what they really wanted. We reviewed their goals, and the deeper I got with them, I learned that they disliked their jobs, and the commute was killing them.

Even though they planned on working five more years, I knew it was important to take a look and make changes because the stress of their lifestyle was affecting their health now. They weren't living where they wanted to, and so many hours a year in a negative work environment was sucking the life out of them. All of that affected other areas in their life as well. After a close review, we discovered that they could retire right away, if they wanted to. Based on their lifestyle expenses and the income sources they had, in addition to the conservative projections I'd done, I told them as long as their lifestyle expenses were accurate and consistent, retiring right away was realistic.

They confirmed that the numbers were accurate. I remember their reactions; they were so surprised, almost in disbelief that they could retire right then. They'd thought they'd just have to continue slugging it out for another five years before they were free. They'd never had a proper financial evaluation done before. I helped them see that they had other choices and I will never forget the reaction on their faces that day.

Within a few days, they decided to sell their house and go find a new home by the water, which had always been a dream of theirs. It was less than twelve months before their dream became a reality. They retired over four years earlier than they had planned to; they are tremendously happier, and loving life so much more.

Most of my long term clients have been in situations where my services became invaluable to them because of the wisdom I was able to offer them when their lives changed. We don't know when change will occur, we just know that inevitably, it will. The model I use directs that myself and my team need to reach out and have frequent contact with our clients; paying attention to cues about things that are going on in their lives. Many times they don't realize they are heading down a pathway to a transition, but because we've gone down this road so many times with others, we are quick to pick up on life change indicators not obvious to them, and we can then start helping them prepare for whatever comes ahead.

Another of the fundamental aspects of my financial advising is the retirement coaching service I offer, which is unique. I take clients through a set of discovery exercises and tools. Not all retirees are created equal, and it's important to talk about their vision and individual goals and desires, which are unique to them. My process and tools help identify those, and the profile I help them create is simply a window into how their individual identities relate to leisure, work, connecting and socializing with others, and self-renewal.

Most people do more planning for a two week vacation than they do for their entire retirement. It sounds crazy, but it's true. Many people think that when they retire, they just stop working. Retirement is a huge change; everything shifts- a person's daily routine, their schedule, their socialization, and more.

People know what they are retiring from, but it hasn't really occurred to many of them to think about what they are retiring to. I get deep with this subject when I help my clients envision what retirement actually looks like. I run them through a mock week in retirement to give them an idea of what the experience is like and how they'll fill their time. I have travelled the globe researching retirees and have helped hundreds of people retire well. This experience has allowed me to help people enter this new chapter in their life with confidence and excitement.

It's definitely not just about having enough money to live in retirement; it's about so much more than that, and I love helping people explore the new lifestyles they will be stepping into. Retirement can have many different forms. To retire means to withdraw to or from a particular place so it doesn't necessarily mean stop working all together. It can lead to new and unexpected roads.

One of my clients was a woman in her late thirties. She had a career she hated; it was shift work, and it was eating away at her. Her husband had the same kind of schedule which made it challenging to raise their kids. She told me that she had a ten year plan; she'd do the shift work for a decade to support the family, and then transfer into a different career; something she'd much rather be doing instead, that would give her some of her time back.

I suggested she change her career right away, going into a sales position that dovetailed with the kind of work she had been doing. She admitted that she hadn't even considered changing careers, but that she'd be interested in it, so she gave it a try. She began working in the new position part-time, while maintaining her prior job, to see if it could work. Everything changed for the better so quickly that she made the full transition to the new job, leaving the old one behind.

We reviewed her situation six months later, and she said that she was doing so well. We turned her ten year plan into an eighteen month plan, and in doing so, gave her a new life. Her schedule became her own, and she no longer works holidays or evenings. Her family has her back, and she's much happier. She's shared with me that she's grateful that I pushed her to do it, because she never would have done it by herself.

There are many success stories, but they come about because people took the time to look at their situations and make changes. Many people focus on long term plans, but those are safety mechanisms. They push their goals out really far into the future, which enables them to avoid taking any action in the present. I ask people when they say they have five or ten year goals; why not act now? Who knows where you'll be in ten years?

If someone had told me that I was going to be a fire fighter, then a paramedic, and then that I was going to own my own financial firm, I wouldn't have believed it. We all experience so many changes in life; so many transitions. That's why it's imperative to sit down with an advisor and look at immediate plans. The average person will go through about sixty transitions in their lives, with the majority of those happening in adulthood, so they need that voice of wisdom to be there to help guide them through those transitions; to be a sounding board. Money goes into motion when life goes into transition, and when that happens, I am there to help my clients with each pathway leading up to their transition.

Many of the people I talk with have no idea what they truly want out of life. If I can help them identify what's most important to them, give them a plan and hold them accountable to it and I make sure that we look through that lens each and every time I meet with them, then I can set them on a path to their own personal best lives.

I want people to know that this is a different approach. It's outside the box. Very few people leave their financial advisors because it's a relationship they've had for so long that they can't bring themselves to overcome the awkwardness of calling up that advisor to tell them they're leaving. People will get a second opinion on their health, but they're apprehensive to get a second opinion on their lifestyle plans. It's vital for people to get out there and get a second opinion, because there are so many different types of advisors out there. If your advisor is only talking to you about investments and the re-

turns on your mutual funds, then you need to be looking at other resources. There's so much more for people
to have; people who want more than just a simple rate
of return on a piece of paper from their portfolio.

I tell my clients when they are off track or on track along
the journey. Everyone needs this extremely important
resource in their life. Getting the best life with the money you have is a necessity, not a want. My clients ask me
many questions and keep me in the loop about what is
going on in their lives, and it helps me to help them
make the changes they need to so that they're living
their best lives right now, and not several years down
the road. For me that's so much better than hey, I got
you an extra 1 or 2% return on your investments last
year'.

I tell people my role is to be their BFF; their best financial friend. When they have life changes, questions, or
concerns, they call me, and we look at things together.
It's all about relationships and doing 100% the right
thing, being as transparent as possible, and simplifying
the intricacies of life.

We live in a world of ever-increasing convolution; we
have less time and more things on our plates. People
need a resource they can trust; someone who can sim-
plify the complex, help them get through their life transitions, and be there as a voice of wisdom for them.

These tools and programs work; my life wasn't perfect
before, but I'm enjoying it so much more now, and I'm
the happiest I've ever been. When I've put myself

through the program that I use for my clients, my scores are high in every category.

I like to tell people, 'Enjoy yourself, it's later than you think!' This is not a practice life or dress rehearsal, so learn to live now with the wealth you have, and at the same time take steps to secure your future.

My business is about showing up for people and helping them make their own lives the best they can be. In my other careers, I was saving people. I'm still saving people; I'm just saving them in a different way.

Then a Pandemic Hits

Here is what I have learned from a business perspective:

1. Many of our actions create the opposite effect of what we want. For example, we work to make money to buy material things that are not needed. But if we don't buy as many material things, we don't need to work as much and will have less money stress and more time to spend with family. I have had many clients tell me how much money they have saved due to the biggest time-out the world has ever had. They were not able to buy non-essential items as easily during this pandemic so it really made people only spend money on what was necessary. At the same time, it gave them the opportunity to realize that buying negotiable items is not what truly makes them happy; it is time with family and experiences that makes them happy.

I hosted a podcast on this topic in May 2020 and you can find it here:

https://theridelifeworkandwealth.blubrry.net/2020/05/06/episode-4-how-do-you-want-to-live-your-life/

2. Many of us were caught on a proverbial hamster wheel of working too much and making life more complex than what is needed. We didn't mean to complicate things, we just got caught up and 'numb' to how we are doing things which are not necessarily improving our lives. Many of my clients have said they are changing their work environment going forward after this.

3. This has been a big opportunity to take two steps back on our lives and ask ourselves 'How do I want my life to look as I move forward?' There has never been a larger time-out on people's lives and I believe this has been an opportunity to reset, reflect, and revisit how we were doing things in our lives pre-Covid 19 and how we want to change things for the better in our lives post Covid 19. As Winston Churchill states "don't waste a good crisis". I realize that many lives have been lost and people have lost their jobs and their businesses. This pandemic has been devastating to many. But amidst all the stress, anxiety and loss, there has also been time to reflect. We can try to take that as a positive repercussion of this crisis.

About the Author

Kris Dureau, CFP, CHS, CCS

CERTIFIED FINANCIAL PLANNER™

Kris Dureau took a unique route into the financial services industry — a route that exemplifies his passion for helping and protecting people. Kris comes from a background in emergency services and has trained extensively in assisting people in emergency situations. Combined with his training in the financial services industry, Kris has incorporated this helping-and-protecting approach into the planning he does for clients.

Serving as an independent financial advisor since 2007, Kris has had a great deal of experience in working with retirees, business owners, and families.

Kris was the second person in Canada to achieve the Certified Cashflow Specialist™ designation. He also holds the CERTIFIED FINANCIAL PLANNER™ and Certified Health Specialist designations. Kris has completed the Canadian Securities Course, Life License Qualification Program, and the Canadian Investment Funds Course.

Kris volunteers as an instructor for the Dollars With Sense program, which teaches grade 7 students about personal finances. He enjoys the outdoors and using the family ATV and Seadoo, playing his guitar and martial arts.

Kris and his wife, Tina, of over 15 years have three young children: Taylor, Chase, Brooklyn, and their fourth child is their rescue puppy, Beau.

He enjoys the outdoors and cottage life, attending all of his kids' activities and sports, playing guitar and practicing martial arts with his kids.

Connect with Kris:

Website: https://www.threehatsfinancial.ca

Podcast: https://theridelifeworkandwealth.blubrry.net

Linked In: https://www.linkedin.com/in/krisdureau

Facebook:
https://www.facebook.com/ThreeHatsFinancial

CHAPTER EIGHT

You Have to be ALL in to Win... and Other Lessons I've Learned as a REALTOR®

By Krystal Lee Moore Lucier

Do you ever find yourself wondering why some people succeed in the face of life's circumstances while others in the same situation end up on the news?

Do you hear the success stories of people and think that it would be next to impossible to be like them?

For me, failure has never been on my radar. I have had big hopes and big dreams since I was a small child and it truly never occurred to me that I would encounter any obstacle that I couldn't overcome.

When I consider the blessings in my life, I am filled with gratitude. I get to wake up every day and guide people through one of the most stressful experiences of their lives – buying and selling homes. I get to be their trusted advisor through the entire process and beyond. I get to stay connected with them and keep in touch with calls, with notes and with pop-by visits. And I get to live my passion and give back to the community and the world at the same time.

And when I look back at my journey so far - the bumps, the ups, the downs and the sharp left turns - it seems to make sense. God's plans for my life are something that I am still uncovering piece by piece, day by day. There have been amazing guides I have been fortunate enough to listen to, to follow, to be mentored by. Coaches who have taken the time to help me. The family I have been blessed with, the friendships that have adorned my experience and the quest for deep and meaningful love which has fueled my life. All of it, all of them, and every moment, has been preparing for today. And every day moving forward. Hindsight is 20/20 though.

"She is so adaptable."

"She fits in everywhere"

"How does she stay so motivated and upbeat?"

"Where does she get her energy?"

I have always been a happy person. Seemingly happier than most people, and definitely unique and outside of what I have observed as normal. And while I have mastered being able to "fit in" anywhere, be it a new city, a new country or a new company, I also never quite feel that sense of belonging that I have craved for as long as I can remember.

Our values are shaped by our lives, our dreams, our passions and our experiences.

One of my strongest values is that of LOYALTY. I am fiercely loyal to my clients, to my friends, my family, my brokerage and any sense of true belonging I can find. And it makes sense. If my aim has always been to feel like I belong and I have desired to be a part of something, it would take BIG things to have me remove myself from a situation or change things up.

And yet change has been the one constant in my 39 years.

One of the questions I am asked frequently is, "How did you get into real estate?"

People are always curious. And it makes sense. Real estate is one of those professions. If you meet 1000 agents, chances are they came from 1000 different paths. We also have this social idea of the typical real estate agent and it's not very flattering. They are pushy. They are phony. And they do not care about anything but that fancy commission cheque and their Bluetooth earpieces.

But there are so many of us who are NOT like that – though even I will poke fun at my colleagues who cannot take that earpiece out.

"Calm down, John. You're not a doctor."

My career goals have varied over the years. As a young child, I decided that I would be a lawyer and a doctor during the week and a judge on the weekends. So, on some level, I guess I always knew I would find a career that had me working weekends.

As I went through high school and university, while working part-time as a cosmetician at Shoppers Drug Mart with a sales focus, I found myself leaning into legal studies (I graduated from Carleton University with a B.A. Honours in Law) and film studies (I had adored theatre as a teenager and stepped away from it later in high school).

I spent seven years working in the legal field, initially in my very first grown-up, full-time job as the Assistant to the Business Manager at an Ottawa law firm named, at the time, Lang Michener LLP (now called McMillan LLP) and then as an Employment Law and Marketing Clerk at another Ottawa law firm named Soloway Wright LLP.

At around the same time, I bought my first home. The real estate agent who helped with the transaction was nice, but we didn't really know each other very well. I will forever be thankful to him, however, because he said something to me that changed my life:

"You should become a real estate agent."

Nope. That was my immediate reaction. I did not want to hear any more. I did not want a career in real estate sales! But he planted a seed. So I decided to peek at the OREA (Ontario Real Estate Association) website. As it turned out, I had ALL of the characteristics one needed to be great at real estate. I decided to take my first course, just to see how it went. I passed.

Then I took the second course. I passed again. And then I took my third course – and even used precious vacation days for it. And I passed.

Whoa.

And I thought I knew exactly where I wanted to work.

I decided that I wanted to work for a specific person and company. I just KNEW it was the right fit. I was so excited. I set up the first interview as soon as I passed my last exam. And it went SO well! I was asked to do something called a DISC test, so I did. And the results came back. As it turned out, I was an ID (Influence and Dominance) – in other words, I was the ideal person for the job.

And that was when I learned one of my first KEY lessons about business:

Beware of those who are threatened by you.

A "friend" had a discussion with the owner of the company on my behalf. There was "no way" that I was an "ID". No way. I would NOT make a good salesperson and, in fact, it would be a bad business decision to hire me. The owner listened to him. And that was the end of that.

To put it mildly, I was crushed.

So, I found a seemingly good Plan B. I allowed another friend (see the theme) to mentor me in a brokerage system whereby he got paid for my production for the rest of my time with the brokerage. I still believe he meant well, but as it turned out, it wasn't a good fit. And I was still a part-time agent because I was a full-time law clerk.

That was when life stepped in – in a big way.

I had gotten married around the same time that I got my real estate licence started. And while he was a great person, we were just not right for each other and truly should never have taken that step. We tried hard, but in the end it just did not work.

I needed to get out of Ottawa, the city I had grown up in. I was struggling with family, my demanding law firm job and well-meaning and kind, albeit slightly workaholic, boss who had me anxiety-ridden, my circle of friends had shifted, and my marriage was over. I would have taken any escape available to me.

And I did.

I met someone. At a real estate conference, of all places. And, like anyone who was struggling and looking for a way out, I ignored everything I saw when I first met him. I let myself believe that he was a wonderful man, who truly cared about me and would be the answer to my life's current despair. In truth, I wanted to be seen. I needed to feel loved, after years of feeling almost invisible. And, maybe most importantly of all, I needed a valid reason to run.

Enter the small town of Guelph, Ontario.

My sister had gone to the University of Guelph. I had been there to watch her in musicals in the War Memorial Hall, and we had eaten at East Side Mario's across from the Stone Road Mall.

That was all I knew of Guelph.

And then I moved there for a relationship that was never going to work. And, after a fairly short and stressful time, it inevitably ended. Looking back, this ending was the very best thing that could have happened to me. At the time, however, it was a devastating turn of events in my new, still somewhat foreign city.

But as I found myself in this desperate situation, far away from almost everyone I knew and cared about and everything that was familiar, something began to happen.

I want to be clear that it did not feel like a magical time. Life throws us curveballs to help us grow and get stronger. And it was a HARD time.

I found myself unsure of what I was trying to do as a real estate agent in this still unfamiliar city with a very small network of acquaintances. I was exhausted. And I was sick of trying to convince people that I was good at helping people with real estate. I wanted to quit so many times. But I didn't.

How did it all turn around, you might be wondering?

How did I go from not selling a single property for 8 months when I started at Royal Lepage in Guelph, to becoming a multi-award-winning Real Estate Broker with amazing clients, friends and colleagues 8 years later? To travelling all over the world? To speaking in cities and attending world class real estate conferences in Canada and the United States, and networking with friends and colleagues all over North America?

How? Let me break it down.

The two most impactful statements that have influenced my career have been:

IF THEY CAN DO IT, I CAN DO IT

I DID IT BEFORE, I CAN DO IT AGAIN

- Brian Buffini, Buffini and Company, Carlsbad California

Seeking to serve others and to promote justice and fairness also fell in my core values of service and justice, so it makes sense that I would enter into a career that would allow me ample opportunity to serve my clients, my colleagues, my network and, through philanthropic endeavors, the world around me. As I progressed down the career path of being a real estate professional, I was blessed with training and lessons from so many sources.

Royal Lepage Canada promotes the Brian Buffini Company and systems to its agents, and when I joined while being new to the city, new to the company, and new to being a full-time real estate agent in 2012, I registered for their program at the time, Peak Producers (now a program called Pathway to Mastery has replaced this). It would be an understatement to say that I was not the happiest camper about this training.

Don't get me wrong: Brian Buffini and his company are amazing. They are phenomenal. They are all about leveraging your database and the people you know to become a successful, giving, happy, and balanced real estate agent and business owner. However, it is difficult to leverage a database of people when you do not have one. Especially when you do not know anyone at all. And even more especially when you have not fully committed to either the city or the career you are in.

Key Lesson Number 2: You need to be ALL IN if you want your business to THRIVE

My adversity in Guelph for the first 8 months became an amazing journey to my success. I needed to experience the humbling reality that a successful relationship-based business comes when you have a strong network of people who know you, who like you, and who trust you. I have always been incredibly coachable and have taken advice from colleagues I respect. One of the agents I worked with in Ottawa was always available to offer his guidance and support when I needed it. And boy did I need it then!

I remember complaining to him one day that nobody in Guelph knew me and that it was impossible for me to do real estate there.

"Well, that is their fault, Krystal. They should all know everything about you because you have grown up there, made friends and connections and spent time and effort getting to know them too."

He was being incredibly pointed and forced me to say out loud what I needed to focus on.

"I am new here and it's not their fault they don't know me. How do I fix it??"

He suggested that I create a video explaining who I was – I opted for a pamphlet and I gave it out at open houses, trade shows and to all of my clients, new networking connections and, basically, to anyone who would take it. I would introduce myself, give a 30 second blurb about who I was, and then encourage them to review the pamphlet later. It was a hit.

I have learned in my career path that the ones to emulate and the ones to listen to are those willing to share – those with a mentality of abundance, and not scarcity. Those who are afraid to share for fear of losing market share are not the people I want to follow.

We also highlighted a few things about my "business".

1. Firstly, I still hadn't fully adopted a new phone number. I was using an Ottawa phone number as my main line and a Guelph phone number as a backup. This had to stop.

2. I also needed to make a decision. I decided to give real estate a FULL year of my undivided attention. I would no longer be an Ottawa Marketing and Law Clerk trying out Guelph Real Estate. I was ALL in.

And, looking back, those two changes made a HUGE difference. That was when I actually started to gain traction and sell homes and build my name as YOUR Guelph REALTOR® Krystal Moore.

As I began to grow, I was trying to keep my database organized on an old-school Excel sheet – for real. My law firm days weren't that far behind me. But it wasn't enough. I needed more.

I tried a free database organizer and it was terrible. Just terrible. And THAT was my lightbulb moment. I remembered that Buffini and Company had a CRM (client referral maker) which was a database. A database I had been able to use for free during my training - and I had never taken advantage of this offer. I signed up for something called "Self-Paced Coaching" to get access to the database. I was plugged into listening to the monthly webinars and audio files that Buffini sent out as well – and started reading some phenomenal personal growth books including:

- *How to Win Friends and Influence People*, Dale Carnegie

- *Think and Grow Rich*, Napoleon Hill

- *The Seven Habits of Highly Effective People*, Stephen Covey

And when I decided to upgrade my membership later that fall to One to One Coaching, everything started to change even more.

Key Lesson Number 3: You should aim to invest 10% of what you PLAN (or hope) to earn into your business.

In 2018, I added a second coaching company to my business - Kathleen Black Coaching Company - and my business is thriving with both organizations. As I have grown my business year after year, my investment in myself, in my business, and in my community has grown substantially. When we start as entrepreneurs, it feels like everyone is asking us to spend more and more money. And while the saying holds true that you have to spend money to make money, it's really hard at the beginning to understand that there is a marked difference between spending money ON your business and investing money INTO your business. That 10% rule is accurate.

If you want to earn more, then you must invest more. Into yourself first, with education and training, into your business, with marketing and the right tools to succeed including coaching and finding the right people to surround yourself with, and finally, into your community by supporting other businesses, people and charities.

- I attend conferences whenever I can, making connections and gaining nuggets of inspiration and wisdom to share with my clients, my colleagues, and my friends and family.

- I read daily, learning from those before me about personal development and business and personal growth.

- I support local charities and participate in global efforts to alleviate poverty and discrimination. It is a huge part of my WHY.

- I take courses to further my career and education whenever possible, and recently obtained my Certified International Property Specialist (CIPS) designation from the Canadian Real Estate Association, of which I am a member. I also serve on the CREA Global Committee to promote international real estate referrals to and from Canada.

- I speak publicly whenever I have the opportunity to, in hopes of educating, inspiring and sharing some of the amazing experiences I have been blessed to have.

- I invest in my business community as well, using an amazing professional stager to prepare and present the homes I list, a professional photographer to show the homes in their best light, a professional cleaner to assist in showing the homes at their best, and a handyperson to help us with that never-ending list homeowners tend to have of things that should have been fixed. I refer my clients to real estate lawyers, mortgage specialists, home inspectors, moving companies, plumbers, painters, electricians and so many others.

- I also invest in my business with local services, from business cards to banners, to my personal insurance needs, home renovation and legal services, to name but a few.

Key Lesson Number 4: Anything you have overcome is now something you can leverage and create AGAIN

After my very steep and very difficult learning curve when I relocated to Guelph, and making the decision to stay there, I decided that I would NOT move again. This would be my home from now on. And I certainly would not move for love, real or perceived, ever again.

You know that saying about how we make God laugh by telling him our plans? He had another path in mind for me.

In 2017, I began to date a very sweet and very handsome man. This man, Brett, lived in another city. He lived in London, Ontario - just 120km down the 401 West from Guelph. And as things progressed and we grew closer, I began to spend more and more time in London. I was happy with the back and forth. Things were wonderful.

And then, in February 2019, this handsome and sweet man took me away to Nashville, TN, for my birthday and got down on one knee and asked me to share the rest of his life with him and his two amazing children. In London.

Well, all I can say is that I didn't plan to EVER meet anyone as amazing as he is. And his love and the new plan have both become central parts of my life.

For over two years, I worked with both of my coaches, Darrin Jackson and Ronn James, to serve both Guelph AND London under the wonderful and safe Royal Lepage banner and still making that 120km drive.

In the Fall of 2020, I made the move officially and joined London's Royal Lepage Triland Realty Brokerage. It's 11 minutes from my new home, versus 1 hour and 20 minutes. I love my Mazda CX-3 – but I needed a break from the 401!

The best part, according to my KBCC coach, Ronn, is that I have already DONE what I am trying to do in London. I have the template, I have the experience, and I am supported by amazing people in the London community. And my Guelph community has been incredibly supportive and amazing throughout the entire process – as they have since the beginning.

I love to guide people through the real estate process, from start to finish. To educate them about what to expect, and to navigate the process with them with my expertise, care, experience and, of course, my ability to bring their stress down to a manageable level.

I also love to share with my colleagues and network the wonderful lessons I get to learn and the systems to help with their success as well.

My career path is far from at its end and my journey is something that truly excites me. The learning, the growth, the serving and the ability to truly impact the lives of those around me in a career that I love is all such a GIFT. It is not always easy. And some days feel like a parade, while some feel like a rollercoaster of emotion. But THAT is why surrounding ourselves with amazingly supportive people who share our values is so very important.

There are those that come and go in different seasons, but the ones who share our values, who are right next to us in the race, and who are there with open arms when we need a friend? Those are my people – and it feels so good to know that I am one of them. I am Krystal Lee Moore Lucier – I am HOME and I belong. At last.

Then a Pandemic Hits

When the Covid-19 pandemic hit, I was asked if there was anything I would have done differently in business. I truly don't think I would have. I believe that I needed to do everything I did to create the business I have. And I am fortunate enough to have created a successful virtual/online business because of technology and my needs in the last few years. Each lesson I learned along the way, even the hard and costly ones, brought me closer to my success today, just as the ones I am learning now will bring me closer to my tomorrow.

The top lessons that I had to learn personally, and which may serve to help others who come after me, are most certainly shareworthy:

1. Determine your Values before doing ANYTHING else in your life. Right now. Today. Find a course online, find a simple exercise or just find a list of values and rank them. Ask yourself the hard questions and figure out what your CORE values actually are. And then look at everyone and everything around you and see if they fit, or where they differ. Understanding why you think/act the way you do AND why others do the things they do will save you countless hours of confusion and frustration in life. Once I figured out MY values, 6 ½ years into my career as a Realtor®, it changed my life in the best way.

2. Find the BEST way to be your BEST authentic self: There are many, many, MANY, books, articles, courses and seminars out there claiming to have found the best way to do business. They are all right. And they are all wrong. You need to get behind a system and an organization that shares your values (this is KEY) and then follow their guidance in your own way. Do what you are BEST at and you will consistently produce your best results.

3. Some people won't like you. In fact, millions of people won't like you. (Calm down, it's going to be okay.) Thousands of people, though, WILL like you. Stop putting time, energy, love and effort in-

to those who do not value or like you. They are not worth it. They are NOT your Avatar. And they are NOT thinking about you. Put your time, love, energy and effort into the ones who DO value you and appreciate you and like you. Your life will head in amazing directions.

At the end of the day, we are all learning. Perhaps I would have gone all in sooner, updated my website professionally or started promoting in different ways, but at the end of the day, it all happened the way God intended it to. I am surrounded by amazing people, both personally and professionally, and I am so grateful for my business and for my Life and excited to share it.

About the Author

Krystal Lee Moore is YOUR #HomeSweet Home 519 REALTOR®, Real Estate Broker with Royal Lepage Triland Realty, Brokerage.

Krystal became a Londoner in 2019 when she very happily married into the Forest City and became Mrs. Brett Lucier.

Specializing in working with First Time Buyers and First Time Sellers in London, Guelph and Surrounding areas, Ontario, Krystal is committed to helping others, negotiating for her clients and to reducing the stress and confusion that often accompanies real estate transactions. Her unique background and education in law and customer service helps to break down the potentially confusing process of selling/buying and allows clients to focus on the exciting adventure ahead.

Krystal is bilingual in English and French, and is connected with several amazing business owners and charitable organizations in London and Guelph, as well as amazing Real Estate agents all over North America.

Krystal holds a B.A. Honours degree from Carleton University in Law, her Real Estate Broker's Licence and is a Certified International Property Specialist. She enjoys World Travel, Mission work, volunteering and is an active Philanthropist for several key organizations including International Teams, with a focus on PACE in Kenya, Big Brothers Big Sisters of London and Area, Youth Opportunities Limited and Childcan in London and Michael House in Guelph.

Connect with Krystal:

www.KrystalMoore.com

www.facebook.com/KrystalMooreRealEstateSales

www.facebook.com/GuelphFirstTimeHomeBuyers

www.facebook.com/LdnOntFirstTimeHomeBuyers

Twitter: @KrystalLeeMoore

Instagram: @yourhomesweethome519realtor

CHAPTER NINE

Surely By Now I'd Have Figured It all Out

"You never know how strong you are until being strong is the only choice you have" – Bob Marley

By Janine Taylor

This quote resonates with me to the point that it feels as though it's become part of my DNA. From as far back as I can remember I've been tackling life's challenges...often not because I felt compelled to, or was being directed or guided to, but because I simply had no choice in the matter.

My earliest memory of my childhood is leaving the only hometown, home and school I'd ever known at the age of 6. I remember my dad picking me up from South Perth Public School in St. Mary's, Ontario, on a sunny May day, which also happened to be the day of our annual school carnival, and telling me to say goodbye to my friends because we were moving. In one afternoon, my entire world as I knew it was about to change. My parents had sold all of our belongings, and with my sister of 4 years of age and my brother not quite 2, we embarked on a cross-country trek to British Columbia where we would eventually settle in Prince George.

Prince George in 1975 was somewhat of an early settled 'dust bowl' in Northern BC. Incredibly remote, it was surrounded by forests with just one highway in and out of the very small city. However, with a population of approximately 59,000, it was a lot bigger than the small town of St. Mary's, Ontario, which was about a tenth of the size. The journey to British Columbia and eventually Prince George was not done in a straight line either. We travelled to Prince George, then Vancouver, where I'm told and vaguely remember my father debating his next career choice, having left an insurance salesman job behind in Ontario, and then going back to Prince George. I vaguely remember the time in Vancouver being spent in Stanley Park as my young parents debated our future, only to return to Prince George and camp in the backyard of an acquaintance while my dad settled into another insurance sales job, and attempted to put down roots in the new city. Thankfully my mom was a registered nurse, and in 1975 that was an asset because she could and would find work easily. After finding us a home, and not a moment too soon as winter temperatures arrive early in Northern BC, we moved into what would be our first of two homes in BC. We were neighboured only by the bears that would frequent the empty lot across the street and several other newly built homes that were scattered on Imperial Crescent.

We only spent five years in British Columbia, but in those short five years I would have to face many challenges as a young person. We moved twice, I was enrolled in three different schools, I fractured several vertebrae along my spine for no specific reason, spent months in a body cast, and suffered from abuse from a family friend that I would continue to struggle and cope with later in life. I would also develop Obsessive Compulsive Disorder (OCD) as a means of coping with the pain, suffering, and sadness I was facing as a young 7, 8, 9-year-old little girl. Of course I didn't know that's what I had, OCD...I only knew that I had to perform these rituals daily, nightly, and spent countless hours breaking down words and syllables in my head because deep down it somehow helped with the emotions and struggles I was dealing with.

British Columbia turned out to have both blessings and curses for me and I have both good and tragic memories of our time spent out west. In some ways we were blessed to have restless parents, because that meant lots of road trips, camping and seeing many aspects of what both BC and Alberta had to offer, and we were fortunate to experience a lot of what the provinces had recreationally as well. For that I was blessed. However, having to change schools three times, cope with such a significant injury, isolation as a result of that injury, abuse and trauma and subsequent suffering in silence, all the while trying to manage it as my OCD worsened, was the curse of my time there. And unfortunately, returning to Ontario in 1980 didn't bring any relief. It was only the beginning of what would be a lifelong course of struggle, challenges, pain, suffering, and the constant effort to overcome them.

I barely remember the decision that was made for our family to return home to St. Mary's in Ontario in 1980. We moved in with my grandma and grandpa in the May of 1980 and I was about to start my fifth school in six years. My OCD had continued to worsen, and as I now know, my anxiety had led way to ticks over the years and now I suffered from depression and regular migraines. In 1980, despite the fact my mom was a nurse, there wasn't a lot of awareness around any of these diseases or afflictions - especially in children. So often I had to suffer alone. In fact, outside of the broken back and migraines, I'm not sure my parents knew much else of my suffering. Don't misunderstand me; my Mom would put hot cloths on my forehead to ease any pain I felt from regular migraines and often allowed me to skip school if I just wasn't up to attending. Looking back, she attended to me with the attention of a nurse and always made me feel safe and in good hands, so to speak. If I needed anything, I knew I could ask her. But I don't know that she ever knew the depths of my pain and sadness. My dad was no help either; I had an arm's length relationship with him for so many reasons. These years set a course for me of which I had no idea the significance until much later in life.

The reality is I would spend my grade school years in six different schools in eight years. The irony in all of this was many of the people, especially the young girls I met throughout those grade school years in Ontario, would eventually become lifelong friends. But it didn't happen for a few more years to come. By the time I entered grade 9, I was a withdrawn, shy girl whose hair was long but purposely hung in front of her face. I look back at pictures from that time and see someone who shied away from the camera and often my face is hidden. I have such sadness in my eyes, and I stand almost hunched over. I'm sure the hunching over was both physical after breaking my back but also emotional, as if I could literally make myself disappear if I just tried hard enough. We moved to a pig farm, and my parents suffered through the tough economic times of the 80's as farmers in Ontario, and eventually we were forced to leave with just one car and the clothes on our back and some furniture. The years on the farm, like everything else in my life to that point, had both blessings and curses. I would experience sexual trauma from a stranger for the second time in my life while living there. I would also face an intruder as I was alone babysitting.

But I would also learn to drive at 14, and a standard transmission at that. I would know what it was to attend youth groups and become part of a community. And I would learn life skills about money and hard work, and understand that decisions could have life-altering repercussions. It was those skills that I would carry with me the rest of my life as I watched my parents struggle and work hard trying to make ends meet, while managing their farm business and the responsibilities that entailed. My parents had strong work ethics. Those years on the farm were not easy. From 1980 until about 1984 we struggled a lot. I think being the oldest I was far more aware of those struggles. Even though I was still very young, I was always very aware. Seeing both my parents spend many late nights at our wooden kitchen table over a ledger, as if staring at the numbers long enough would change the overall bottom line, brought about new anxieties in me and a feeling of sadness and empathy but if I'm being completely honest, it also brought resentment.

I didn't know it at the time, but I believe my Dad struggled with depression most of his life. He was always searching to fill a void he felt somewhere deep within him. He walked away from a partnership in a highly successful auto insurance agency in Prince George, only to sink the hundreds of thousands of dollars in savings and profits he'd returned from BC with into a Mennonite pig farm at the beginning of what would be the toughest economic times farmers would ever see in Ontario. But as the young 12- year-old girl, I knew we'd left a home in a good neighbourhood in remote BC with a comfortable life, to a farmhouse that needed a lot of work and which was turquoise blue...outside and in, everywhere. The soot from the oil burning lamps the Mennonites used stained every wall. The smells of the oil and the scent of the barn and pigs was ingrained in every inch of that house. The kitchen floors were quite slanted, so if you dropped something it would roll several feet before stopping. My dad left a good job in BC to pursue what I can only imagine was an unrealistic dream to become a pig farmer despite the fact he knew nothing of pigs, or farming. I'll never fully understand my dad's decision to do this...and it was my dad steering the ship at that time. However it did teach me many valuable lessons I would carry with me for years to come. Many of those lessons I didn't even learn or realize until I was much older.

Entering high school was tough, but thankfully the way I entered was not the way I left. The withdrawn, shy, somewhat broken girl who entered high school is not the girl that went to college after Grade 13.

Thankfully I met a wonderful young woman, who I will refer to as Kate, in grade 10 through our mothers, who worked together as nurses. She brought me out of my shell and gave me the opportunity to reconnect, and essentially re-introduce myself to many of the young people I'd encountered on my public school journey at different schools. And, as with many young teenagers, I was fortunate to enjoy teenage years filled with parties, drinking, boys, adventures, heartbreak and lots of joy. Between grades 11 and grade 13, I would have to say those were some of the happiest years in my life. Unfortunately, the universe wasn't prepared to give me an easy road to travel so those happier years were short-lived. But I always look back on them with such warmth and a sense of contentment. I was still struggling with my inner demons, but the distractions of teenage antics helped keep them buried deep.

As I left for college in 1987 to follow in my mother's footsteps of becoming a nurse, I had no idea what the next three decades would bring. I was only at college one year before I had what could have been a fatal accident one April day. I was driving and after hitting a soft shoulder on a road with sharp bends, we flew through the air end-to-end and then flipped side-to-side 4 times. I had 3 friends with me at the time; one of my closest male friends was in the passenger seat beside me and by nothing short of a miracle we all survived. I cannot lie and say I learned what it was like to come close to death that day because the truth of the matter is I was young, ignorant to a degree, and didn't fully take in the reality of that accident for some time to come. My actions led to a careless driving charge and had it not been for my Dad insisting just one week later that I get back behind the wheel and drive, it could have changed the course of my life drastically. I would also face another assault at a house party during those years, but I'd become a master at burying any kind of trauma quite deeply. So much so that I barely remember being affected by it at the time. That alone is both alarming and sad. My OCD continued to be like an annoying friend that's always with you, but that you've come to rely on, even if it's not a healthy reliance. I finished my nursing education with both honours and an award in bedside nursing, and I excitedly moved to London, Ontario, to start my dream job as a Neonatal Intensive Care Nurse.

When I moved to London, I was sure I'd be there for many years. I was only 21 at that point but essentially had been on my own, having taken up being a roommate with my grandma during my college breaks in the summer instead of moving back home. I felt as though I'd already been living independently. In more ways than one. Financially, of course, it was such a struggle. I survived on instant rice and frozen corn and Ramen noodles for many meals. Credit card debt, high interest car loans and annoying roommates were the key to surviving those years on my own. But what I wasn't prepared for was what would be a life-changing meeting; the Sunday night of the long weekend in May in Grand Bend in 1991, where at Coco's Bar and Restaurant on Main Street, I'd meet the man who would become my future ex-husband, father of my only beautiful son and business partner for the next 28 plus years.

It was well after 11:30 pm on a night I wasn't even planning on going out, after what had already been a long weekend of partying and drinking. But in walked this tall, very muscular man and I saw him immediately. He was hard to miss because he wore a large jean jacket, no shirt, jeans and a belt that may blind the average person's eyesight. And he certainly didn't fit in with the crowd in Grand Bend. I wasn't sure if he was Greek, perhaps? Maybe Italian? All I knew was he was attractive, and he walked with a confidence you didn't see every day. He was young, I knew that much.... but he walked up to me and after we exchanged a few words, we spent the rest of the night walking the beach, talking and, of course, kissing. I learned he was half Jamaican and half Ukrainian. He was from Mississauga, living in Port Credit, and he was 21. I at the time was 23. We exchanged phone numbers as the sun came up that Monday morning, and by the time I'd returned home to my place in London later that day he'd already left me a message. After going to Port Credit the following weekend to visit him, and spending a weekend together, we would spend the next 3 months driving the 401 between Port Credit and London to spend our time together when I wasn't working my shifts at the hospital and when he wasn't, well, doing what he was doing.

His name was Robert and even at 21 he showed that his keen ability to sell pretty much anything was his God given gift. He was good at it. He certainly sold himself to me! But after just three short months we made the decision to move in together. I got a job without difficulty in Toronto at a major hospital in a good neonatal unit and moved into Robert's apartment where he, I and his roommate lived together.

The next 7 years were filled with a lot of struggle, pain and heartache, but also joy, blessings and a career decision that would prove to be the right one.

I think I had only been living with Robert for about 7 days when I feared I'd made a huge mistake. We'd just had a fight that would begin a cycle of arguing that would continue for the remainder of our relationship until well after our divorce. But at 23, having just moved my entire life to an unknown city, to a new job, living with a young man I barely knew, deep down as hard as it was I felt compelled to stay. I believe the thought of staying and enduring pain and heartache sounded like the easier alternative at the time than getting up and walking out the door. The relationship with Robert almost seemed like we had gotten on a treadmill and couldn't get off. Within 3 months of meeting, we moved in together.

Within 6 months we had already ventured into business together, doing clear-outs of clothing and merchandise and selling them at the Exhibition, Sportsman Show and other local shows and markets. I followed Rob's lead and I was a very fast learner. His negotiation and sales skills, coupled with my logic, common sense and ability to follow direction, seemed to mesh better than our personalities did and far better than the romantic relationship did. We took the cash we made at the shows, and my pay as a nurse, and covered rent, barely, and paid for the necessities, barely.

We used my $1000 moving bonus which was provided to relocate me to Toronto and Robert decided it would be a good idea to start an ice cream waffle business. Being far too naïve, and not yet having found my real voice, I didn't agree to the idea, but I said nothing and he took my silence as compliance. That would be how many of our business ventures would go for years. We struggled a lot during those early years, however still managed to get engaged within 2 years, married within 3, pregnant and baby within 4, and divorced within 7. During that time we moved twice, started what would be our most successful business to date, broke each other's hearts a thousand times and had an amazing son together. And around year 5 I made the decision to leave nursing behind for good, and devote my entire time and energy into our business.

The final decision to leave Robert was not the dramatic scene you may imagine. We'd fought and challenged each other hundreds and hundreds of times. But the reality is, and Robert would agree, that we were both young, and he was very self-centered and not ready truly to carry the responsibilities of husband and fatherhood. And I was still that young girl who never felt like I was good enough. I was insecure and despite how angry I'd get over the unfair workload of both our marriage and at times our business relationship, my complaints often fell on deaf ears. By default, those responsibilities Robert failed to live up to fell on my shoulders and were an incredibly heavy burden at times to carry. After many ultimatums over the years and one last ditch effort to save our marriage, we returned from a cruise shortly after New Year's in 1998, our son a few weeks shy of his 3rd birthday, and for the first time in our relationship I had a strength and calmness come over me when I told Robert I was finally done and I asked him to please move out. He did the next morning; however, the actual separation and divorce were really, really tough. The business we had started in 1992 had been growing, and I didn't see the point in blowing up our marriage and the company. So, we decided to continue to work together. You can imagine a 27 and 29-year-old, trying to navigate a divorce while still going to work together every single day and the toll it would take. Robert coped by dating, partying, and spending money on fast cars and speedboats and I was busy being a mother, business owner. I decided that dating seemed like a good therapy for my broken heart and spirit as well. At 30 years old, without taking any time to heal, I dove right back into the dating pond. I spent time with different guys, in casual relationships, before settling into yet another long-term relationship which would change my romantic life course like no other.

I'm not going to give this person the credit of naming him, and he certainly doesn't deserve more than a paragraph devoted to him. Within 2 years of separating and divorcing from Robert I was living with this other man and he'd become somewhat of a stepfather to my son.

Also during this time, my overall health problems that began in childhood had started to rear their ugliness again. I think I was completely worn down both emotionally and physically and my body chose this time to release the diseases that had lain dormant, ready to come out. In a matter of 18 months, my spine deteriorated to the point that I required major back surgery for fear my spine, if not fused, would lead to paralysis and further compromising of my spinal cord. This was a surgery I wasn't prepared for and it has still left me with problems today. I was diagnosed with a pituitary tumour in my brain and was told I was sterile and had likely been for several years. I could and would have no more children. I was diagnosed with arthritis, severe osteoporosis, narcolepsy, and esophageal ulcers all within a year. I was told that I'd likely be wheelchair-bound by the time I was 50. The pain and nerve damage as a result of my spinal and bone disease was debilitating most days. Throughout this period, I continued to raise my son, virtually with no help, manage a household, maintain a relationship, and work full time with my ex-husband. To say that I felt overwhelmed would be a gross understatement. But the proverbial straw that broke the camel's back? This unnamed man and I were trying to have a baby when we learned the devastating news of my pituitary tumour. He announced to me in May of 2002 that he wanted to be with someone that could have children that would be biologically his. I don't recall much more than that about that conversation. I'm sure I blocked it out as his words were still sitting in the air that day. And for years I've told myself that's why that relationship ended. And it largely was. But if I'm being completely honest, I think we both knew our relationship would never last. It was as if we were in a locked room together and someone decided to open the door a crack and we both took the opportunity to run out that door. The fact that I couldn't have more children, or his child, was just another one of life's cruel jokes.

Or, as I write this today, my now much older self would console my almost 34-year-old self and claim it was likely a blessing. However, once again, I had found myself with a man I knew in my heart was all wrong for me. Within weeks he had moved out. So I sold that home, moved to my current home, and vowed never to enter a relationship with anyone ever again. I've kept that vow....it's the vow I've held the longest, and I'm now 52 years old and have not been in a relationship with anyone since 2002. And while I'm being honest, it occurred to me several years back that I don't think I've ever truly been in love either in my 52 years. I've told several men I love them for sure...including Robert, of course, and this unnamed man we are speaking about. There was my first boyfriend and a wonderful guy I dated before meeting Robert. But I've been told that genuine love is respectful, nurturing, kind, supportive, it feels good, it doesn't hurt, it's not isolating or lonely, it grows, it doesn't take away and overall it feels warm not cold...so I thought that if this is in fact true, then I've never known that kind of love with a man.

At this point in my story you're probably reading this and saying to yourself, this woman has obviously seen her share of pain, heartache and life's challenges, but where is the moral of the story? Where are the life lessons? When does she have the realization that catapults her forward to find true love, continued success in business, spiritual enlightenment?

Well first you may ask, what does a woman who has decided she will never enter a relationship with a man (or woman for that matter), ever again, do with her time? She works.... a lot......and more importantly, I worked at becoming the very best parent to my son that I could be while largely ignoring my own needs and growth for almost 16 years. Since that fateful day in 1992, I started not 1, but 3 businesses with my ex-husband and we also managed to find a good basis for a working relationship and friendship over the years. It's certainly not perfect, but you can't deny that we do well together in business. I raised my son to be a healthy, well-adjusted now 25-year-old young man who also happens to be a talented entrepreneur and one of the warmest, kindest, most caring and funniest human beings I've ever known. Robert and I, today, have found a way to form a modern family unit as he was blessed with another amazing son, 15 years after having his first born, my son's brother, and I'm blessed to have a strong bond with him as well.

I certainly grew into my own when it came to business. It turns out I had a good head and strong instincts for it. My common sense, logical approach to tasks, my thirst for knowledge and inquisitive nature, coupled with a strong work ethic, my nurturing personality, and many of the skills I learned and adopted as a nurse, have allowed me to lead our businesses over the years to find success at times and survive debilitating failures at other times. We managed to survive several recessions and the outright business and often life altering global recession (I'd say depression) of 2008/2009, and not only survived that time but we in fact thrived. I've had the pleasure of being named one of Canada's Top Women Entrepreneurs twice, and had our company named in Profit and Chatelaine magazines as a top growing business in Canada twice. Our second online retail business was a runaway success on Dragon's Den just a year ago, and we were able to finally fulfill a long-term goal and bought a large commercial building a year and a half ago and started what would be our 3rd business – and I have been partnering with my ex-husband for all of it. Collectively our businesses do over $15 million annually in 2019 and today I manage a wonderful team of employees; 30 across all companies. Personally, I have entered back into dating life and it's been filled with many frustrations and loads of fun, and I'm trying to welcome both experiences wholeheartedly. I feel more comfortable in my skin than I have in years. I have friendships today with many of those young girls I felt so isolated from during my primary school years, and am fortunate to have strong bonds with those women that I know will last a lifetime. As it happens, my ability to have more children was taken from me years ago but instead I was presented with so many opportunities, over and over again, to act in a parenting role and I am truly fortunate to have been called "Mom" by over a dozen of my son's closest friends over the past 18 years. And I just became a 'Grandma' as one of those young boys had his first son recently. I know there are going to be many more births, weddings and celebrations I'll be a part of because of these wonderful young people as they venture through their lives.

But, and there's always a but, let's be honest - after reading this, you'd likely agree I'd be a therapist's dream client. They could retire off a few years' sessions with me!
But in all sincerity, my opening quote is often my reality.
I've overcome struggles and found strength when
needed, often because I had no other choice. I can,
however, say this - there is choice in choosing to fight, to
dig deep for any kind of strength, and I've done that
many times. I could have easily succumbed to any one
of my diseases, given in to heartbreak, and let the depression, abuse, losses and failures swallow me up. But I
chose to get up each day and face each and every challenge. There were years where I was so numb I barely
remember time passing. Often when circumstances
were especially tough, or everything in my world felt
quite dark, I'd set goals for myself that were attainable.
Quite a few days, months and years went by where
those goals were no more than: get up, brush teeth,
brush hair, get son to and from school, get him fed,
home and in bed safe, work from home and sleep....
then repeat. And certainly, my decision to live a life of
somewhat solitude, non–traditionally 'alone', without a
relationship or full-time partner, may not be the norm,
but to me it feels as it should be and that decision in
and of itself takes strength. Living your life on your own
without a partner to lean on, share time with, face the
world with, requires a special fortitude. It requires you to
develop a set of skills where you look to yourself, within
yourself for reassurance, reasoning, comfort and security
- and that's not always easy to do. There is nothing that
quite tests your strength more than when you walk
through the door after an unbelievably hellish day of
work, your head filled with thoughts that would frighten

many, and the only person to vent to is yourself. The only person to tell about your day is yourself. And the only person to talk you off the ledge some days is yourself. Not to mention putting on a brave face for your child on so many of those days. Remembering who you are, when it's only your voice you're listening to, can test even the strongest of individuals. Going without another person's touch, sometimes for years, can test your resolve.

As is often the case with life, I had written a different ending to my chapter and as I was finalizing edits, as I literally write this, we are entering another very probable global recession, perhaps depression. We are in the middle of a global pandemic that has infiltrated virtually every country across our globe and is taking lives, while reducing countries and many business economies to their knees. We have seen of late so much unrest. There is a great deal of uncertainty right now as we are going to face financial and personal challenges in the upcoming year. Perhaps it will be greater than any challenge we've ever faced before. How significant; nobody knows.

I needed a new ending and decided to get help. I sent my chapter to a dear friend of mine, Laurie, to review, with the explicit understanding she could also be free to edit it. I trust and respect her opinion a great deal, so her initial assessment was important to me. Her reply, her words not mine, were, "I haven't changed much....but I believe you owe yourself a stronger TRIUMPH ending...I want you to own the true awesomeness that you are and what you have created. You have moved boulders and overcome what others would crumble under. I want to know at the end that you love your life and are feeling joy..." and it was at that last word she lost me, as I laughed under my breath. I thought to myself, joy? That might be a stretch, I thought. And within minutes, I received a follow-up email from Laurie, "Perhaps joy is too strong of a word....", as I laughed to myself again, because yes, she knows me well. But she went on to say "perhaps it's KNOWING...Knowing that you will wake tomorrow to face another battle, knowing that you will triumph through any trial that is brought your way, knowing that you have the internal strength to weather any storm." And as I read her words, I immediately began to think, Yes, it is a knowing. Or maybe more of a feeling, an instinct, that I know will face these upcoming challenges head on and attack them with the perseverance and strength I've had to muster many times before. Yes, in part, I don't have a choice but to persevere, but it's by the sheer fact that I've managed to collect years of experiences and accomplishments through trials and failures that I know that I can and will endure. That is the knowing part. It won't be easy but easy has rarely been in my vocabulary throughout my life. I know that I have my son, who is successful and kind and my proudest achievement. I have family, friends and those friends that have become family to rely on should I need them. I'm thankful for the fact that the doctors were wrong, and I'm not only not in a wheelchair but I'm walking up to 5km effortlessly. That I may not have been able to have more biological children but I'm 'Mom' to so many. I'm thankful that I have a business partner and friend whom I trust wholeheartedly, even though we had a rocky start decades ago. I'm fortunate that my other illnesses are well under control and that I took control of my life in a way even I didn't think was possible. I'm thankful I had the courage to start dating again and I'm aware that I'm a work in progress, but I'm grateful for the journey. And it may not be joy but on many days, you can hear me laughing now because I'm happy. And on a professional front, as we face this crisis, I have also had time to reflect on our businesses and how we may move both through this and recover from it.

Then a Pandemic Hits

I am witnessing so many businesses devastated by the pandemic. And as challenging as our initial lockdowns were, I have reached a somewhat manageable 'new normal' and feel I have learned some very valuable lessons along the way both professionally and personally. Professionally, I have learned the importance of having a business that is scalable so that when times are tougher, scaling back is an option and one that can be implemented quickly. I have learned that having a partner you can trust is more important than always getting along and agreeing. I have learned that people will surprise you in ways you never expected and let you down the same, but it is your response to both that is key. And I have personally learned that I may experience many things in life both personally and professionally, but how I cope and respond to those experiences is often in direct correlation to how I perceive those situations and crises. Just because something negative may happen, it is not a reflection on me personally, or something I may 'deserve'; that my outlook can have a massive impact on how I see a challenge or crisis. And an even larger impact on how I come through it.

About the Author

I am Janine Taylor and I am a young 52 years old. Technically I am 13 birthdays old having been born on February 29th, a leap year. I was born in a small town in St. Marys, Ontario and have spent most of my adult life in the Greater Toronto Area after having re-located here at the young age of 23. I started my career out as a Registered Nurse but after meeting my now ex-husband, found myself in the business world. Over my many years I have had to face challenges both personally and professionally. How I have chosen to face those challenges has shaped not only my psyche but, in many ways, influenced the paths I chose and often found myself on at different stages over the years. Today I am the owner of 3 businesses with that very ex-husband. And the incredibly proud mother of a 25-year-old young man.

Composing this chapter for this book proved to be very cathartic and I can only hope what I learned about myself through the writing process may set me on my next adventure more self aware, stronger and ready to face whatever other trials could and will present themselves. And if by chance my words can provide some insight, comfort, or entertainment to whomever may read them? Then that is a welcomed bonus.

Connect with Janine:

https://www.tntworld.com

CHAPTER TEN

Designing Your Reality

By Tracy Teskey

First, I watched the game. Now, I strive to be in the game.

That's how I feel this journey into becoming a professional businesswoman really started for me. I was raised by a father who drove a tanker truck for Petro Canada before owning his own dump truck business (Teskey Haulage), and my mother paid my way through dance school with her own home-based sewing business, creating the most beautiful dance costumes (thanks Mom). I remember my mother lived by the credo "always be prepared", and her influence rubbed off on me. I never questioned the value of work ethic, knowing that starting my day with my hair done and makeup on was the only way to live - on point and ready to tackle anything and everything that could, and would, come my way.

We all have our heroes, and mine often came in the forms of singers and soap opera stars. I'd rush home from school to soak up VHS recordings of my favourite soaps or MTV Videos. My fixation gravitated towards the strongest, most powerful women on those shows; Lauren Fenmore from The Young and the Restless had my full attention. She embodied it all - strength, sexiness, independence, and a sassy businesswoman vibe that nobody dared mess with.

I already knew at ten years old who I wanted to be, and it was Lauren Fenmore. A businesswoman who dressed up, worked in an office, and knew how to direct and influence people. Or a school teacher - but a very organized one and I would teach math. So, at this point I knew I would need to figure out how to get really good grades and go to University. I worked really hard to get those good grades, and I went on to study Psychology and Business Administration at the University of Waterloo.

I'll humbly confess, to date I've only ever done three interviews in my life; not counting the gas station jobs, or the convenience store positions I held during high school and later University. Each interview culminated in landing the positions that paved the road in my career journey that I had dreamed of as a little girl. I dressed up in smart suits every day, making a point of wearing clothing that was way beyond my years, trying to disguise my baby face behind tailored jackets and shoulder pads. And it worked. The "old boys" took me seriously, and why wouldn't they? I delivered.

I had one goal when I graduated, and that was to be in business. What that meant I wasn't quite sure. I figured I needed to sell something, and to get a corporate sales job I needed some type of experience. So I set about gaining it, dabbling in multi-level marketing during my university years, then selling Mary Kay Cosmetics before replying to an ad in the newspaper selling Kirby vacuum cleaners door to door. I gave my first sales pitch selling online marketing ads for the BBS (Bulletin Board System; "the internet before the internet". Then I volunteered for them during university. Nothing was off limits, because all I wanted was to satisfy my desire to be a businesswoman and become what that hustle and game was all about.

My first interview was in Toronto after responding to an ad in the newspaper for a computer/networking company. This was in 1996 which was good timing for me, since by 1999 every company needed new computers and servers, and with Y2K lurking around the corner work was abundant. I know I got the job because I knew what a hard drive was and how networks worked thanks to my volunteer hours at the BBS.

My second interview happened after I decided to move back to Waterloo, and yes, a boy was involved - a very cute Portuguese bricklayer. That relationship didn't work out, probably because his reaction to my $45,000/year salary plus commission offer was, "That's pretty good for a girl." To say 'that didn't go over well with me' would be an understatement. That moment I channelled 'Lauren Fenmore' and moved on. I took the job and moved back to Waterloo to run the computer & networking division.

I entered the corporate telecommunications world in 2000 after the head hunter who'd found my previous job opened up yet another opportunity. Along came my third interview, and I was offered a position with a $65,000/year salary plus commissions. I thought I'd hit the lottery, to be honest. I was 25, and I remember my dear friend Deen (who now owns and runs her passion project www.chattymonk.com) and I jumping up and down in my office. It was that pivotal moment which would create the trajectory for my 20-year telecommunication career. Year after year, I was winning top sales awards. Presidents Club Awards, Corporate Sales Awards, Leaders Circle Awards. I remember the exclusive Leaders Circle event in Hawaii, and being escorted in black Escalades to a private function that felt very 'lifestyles of the rich and famous,' reserved for only the top-tier players. I had to pinch myself and be in the moment that evening... I had made it. I was a successful businesswoman. Lauren would be proud! I was earning over $300,000/year, loving my home, my pretty Mercedes, and life in general.

I transitioned from Account Executive to Sales Management over the course of 7 years. I was then head hunted again to join one of my largest customers and enter their leadership team. I wanted to try something new and loved 'process and automation', so took on the operations role. Over the next 6 years I ran operations for a national telecommunication carrier, and at the height of my career I was a Chief Operating Officer, residing at the top of the executive ladder and the only woman in the room, but an equal in every way.

Fortunately for me, I instinctively knew how to be a sales person. My psychology training was influential in my early selling days. Listen more than you talk, and create a strong bond based on genuine caring. I hid my self-doubts and kept my mouth shut, sometimes watching others sink themselves after a few drinks by professing their own insecurities. I sat in boardrooms 'pretending' I was on a soap opera and I was the star, and I thrived under the tutelage of powerful women like Laurie Hawkins, my sales manager in my first telecom role, who believed in me. I took every learning opportunity I could get, taking advantage of expensive sales courses offered by the companies I worked for who understood my worth and invested in my abilities.

I considered being a female in a male dominated industry an advantage. When I came to clients with an aura of, "I'm just here to help," they found me hard to turn down, and my chutzpah had me going after the biggest fish in the industry. They couldn't help recognizing that knowledge about computers and tech was in my blood, and my quickness in understanding their problems and delivering a solution gave them all the comfort they needed to say that final "yes."

It isn't all roses in the corporate world, and anyone living in the world of high-pressured sales knows that you lose sleep many nights when the pressure of success is driving you.

This is when the real journey into my new reality began. Sitting in a hammock on top of the world in my vacation home in Costa Rica, reading, "The Monk who sold his Ferrari"... I started to really visualize my own path, and how I could help people plan their dreams and their lives so they could truly live a balanced, happy life.

I knew I had a passion for numbers. I was the nerdy 20 year old staying home on Friday nights, poring over bank statements and creating spreadsheets. I started crafting five-year plans, first for myself, then for anyone who'd let me. Lining up money and life goals became a mission, and I felt a shift start to happen.

But choosing to live for myself was one of the hardest steps I'd take. How do you give up certainty? How do you take a financial hit so you can take a metaphoric leap into the abyss, hoping destiny will catch you?

I was afraid of not having a set salary, afraid of struggling. I'm a "safety" person first and foremost, plus my loyalty towards my company meant I'd hate to put them at a disadvantage. And considering the many hats they put on my head, constantly shifting me into positions that would grow the company even more, how could they live without me?

"Tracy, take on the business division." "Tracy, run the residential division." "Tracy, go deal with our next acquisition." "Tracy, go deal with rolling out a new infrastructure." "Tracy, here's another acquisition." "Tracy, take on the call centre." "Tracy, take over marketing."

I was fixing everything from business sales to taking on new channels and securing those, yet still feeling unful-filled.

But I stayed in the game, with a little bit of a twist. I started my own company alongside our CEO at the time Jody Schnarr, and looking back, I can see how it set me up with the confidence to take the first steps towards running a business on my own terms.

It took four years of co-owning to finally feel like I'd cre-ated a reliable foundation of knowledge. These years forced me to face my fears of being an 'entrepreneur', and that bridge helped me say, "Okay, I really know how to do all the bits and pieces that surround a business."

I'd spent my professional career making a difference in other people's lives, and now it was time to make an impact on my own. I'd always known I loved to help people, and I knew I could make a difference in this world. As my mind married my deep desire to create positive change and my love of number crunching, I re-alized making five-year calendar plans was a pull I could no longer deny. It was time to leap.

In 2019 I branded and developed a business to "Design Your Reality", and started another brand new, five-year plan. I could see the road ahead, mapping out how I'd get to a definition of "retired" that appealed to me. I'm too much of a go-getter to ever sit still, and for me put-ting my feet up meant having four hour workdays and spending four months of the year travelling and working on my laptop. Retirement for me equals making $100K+ a year and having time flexibility.

I'm passionate about helping people to have clarity about what their life should truly be. They say hindsight is 20/20, and I'm stretching my hand out to younger versions of me, saying, "Look, I know the dumb stuff you'll do, and some of the tough decisions you're going to face. You don't need a 5K shopping trip, you need to buy an investment property. You need to map out your next five years, and then the next five after that. You need to believe in yourself."

Creating my own calendars and visualizing how I wanted to be living my life got me off the treadmill. It's so easy to let the years go by, doing the same thing, convincing yourself that this is "success". And there's a certain level of comfort when the corporate world is in control of your life. But the fear I had at 35 has gone away.

Coupled with my vision of where I wanted to go and how I wanted to live my 'week in a life', I recalled what I learned in 2011 watching my life unfold from deep within the trenches when a message came my way via a PBS documentary about Nicholas Tesla. And I'll admit, I feel like I was aligned to "get" this particular message, because my lifelong curiosity about computers and driving ambition put me right in the industry that would play with this very concept day in and day out - we are all frequency, and capable of creating energetic changes in our lives that will shift our futures. All we have to do is understand that Intention (frequency) + Effort (wiring) will always culminate in the outcomes we want. We can make a metaphoric 'wireless' telephone call of our life - if we believe (know the number) and take action (dial).

There is a lot of information now on the internet about frequency. How good we feel, how much closer to our 'true self' we become when we are tapped into our highest frequency. The Happiness Psychology is fascinating, and a lot of the evidence on what makes us feel better is about raising our frequency, or getting our bodies to the optimum frequency level.

I'll try to technically share my theory as it relates to wireless technology. In all fairness, I might lose you here, but the point is this is WHY the calendar planning is so important versus just visualizing life.

The Cell Phone = The Calendars

The Routers/Hardware Devices through the network = Our Human Body

The Wireless Frequency the devices know how to leverage = The Wireless Frequency that our Human Bodies would ideally tap into (this is the difficult part for us humans and why we need tools to try to figure it out).

The Dial Pad on your phone = The Tesla Pens that you write with onto your calendars I'll use Rogers Wireless LTE in Canada as my example.

First Rogers is connected into the frequency and BAND here in Canada (if you're like me and want to go deeper into how this all works, let's have a chat... I'd love to explain it). Your device must be compatible with the Rogers network and the various frequencies and bands used/paid for and configured throughout the networks.

Rogers LTE Frequencies are 700 MHz (Band 12), 1900 MHz (Band 2), 2600 MHz (Band 7), and 1700/2100 MHz AWS (Band4).

Everything from the cell phone you buy in Canada that allows for LTE, to the radios you see on the wireless towers, to the routers and the wireless frequency, must all be configured and 100% inline to allow that cellular telephone, or data transmission, to work properly.

Just like you can make a cellular telephone call, you too can make a life call and put your vision and beliefs out into the universe via our human frequency.

I believe the human frequency is between 62Hz and 72Hz in its optimum state. If we can raise it beyond this - the magic really happens. This is why meditation, listening to music at 432Hz, 528Hz and 963Hz (there are more), laying in a hammock, and connecting with the earth, sun, water and fire - these all increase our human frequency, making us 'feel' better, more confident and like who we just know we are meant to be. This is the energy ideally that you would be feeling when you would re-open your design box... and make that call for your life!

The theory that I believe is that IF we can get our human frequency heightened above 72Hz - we can really make things we believe in strongly happen. Like the LTE cell phone connecting at 700Ghz, the phone call connects, and you hear your friend on the other end of the line. You can make your own call to the universe and design YOUR reality. Amazing, yet so simple really.

Ok - back to the story :)

So I guess technically I'm in the midst of my fourth interview with myself.... and I got the job! I love helping people to "tap into their frequency and open their minds up to the possibilities."

Now it is time to paint you a visual picture. Here's what a typical 'Design Your Reality' experience feels like for my clients.

I set the stage (with purpose to raise their frequency), the candles are burning, the lights are warm, and the tea is ready to be served. I love the feel of a 'tropical spa'; it brings my heart peace, tranquility, and calm and raises my own frequency. I set my own vibration/frequency as my client enters the space to start their 'Design Experience'.

"Alexa, play high frequency relaxing spa music" I instruct, and soft notes fill my house as I make my way towards the front door.

"Hi Nicole! Come on in," I say warmly, as a fiery brunette that I've met at a networking event enters. Her eyes instantly open wide at the scent of sage and Palo Santo wood that I've burned in the air before her arrival. "Wow, your space is so lovely, and smells so nice". My little heart goes pitter-patter and I know I'm taking her into my world and a transformation is about to begin.

We head to the familiar kitchen area, where Nicole selects from the row of teas. "I'm trying this blueberry green tea!" she proclaims, and I put a sachet into a steaming cup of boiled water before we head to my workspace together.

"How are you doing today?" I ask Nicole, picking up my pen and the pad to quietly begin listening to her story and her dreams. I am tapping into designing her ideal week.

"Excited and a bit nervous to actually think about how I want to design the next 5 years of my life," Nicole replies, and I'm gratified to see how much her mood has shifted since we met at the networking event. "I've got to tell you, I was scared when I first started filling in the prework, but I know you're going to help me. Where were you ten years ago, Tracy?" Nicole laughs when I can't help replying, "Waiting for you to be ready for this experience, Nicole!" I actually get a little giddy at this point in the process.

We spend three glorious hours working through her vision, dreams and finances. I can tell she's excited, and I love how optimistic she's become in our short time together.

At the end of the session, she is so calm and the feeling of clarity she feels about her life is palatable. I hand her as her parting gift: her 5 year calendar plan, her magical Tesla pens and her very own 'Design Box', complete with a pretty purple bow.

I know I have found my purpose, passion and love for life.

It was about 3 months later, and Nicole came for her 'deep dive' follow-up session to refine the plan... and before we started I lean forward. "Before we start, how are you enjoying the changes you've been implementing?"

"Seriously Tracy, I thought it was going to be so much harder. But I feel like I've got more time and energy! I've been enjoying my morning routine and paying attention to the little things that make my heart sing. Like I have this healthy coffee at home in the morning now, and it's such a smooth start to my day, plus I've got ten extra minutes for a morning meditation or reading. It's like my mornings are more relaxed, and it really sets the tone for the day. And, notice my outfit? I switched my thinking around shopping for clothes! I'm still loving how I look, but for less money!" She continued on, rattling off a dozen more ways she'd cut into her finances and carved out chunks of money and time for her dream life.

"Thank you, Tracy, seriously. I feel so much better." She leans back a moment, blinking back the sudden tears that come to her eyes. "Free, in fact. I've got this vision for where my life is going and I feel light as a feather every morning when I get up. It's like I can see the future, and it looks amazing. I'm so happy, and it's all because of you."

"Well, you're the one doing the work, Nicole," I reply, blushing at the compliments.

The cool thing for me is to have insight into her dreams and how she is tactfully, with a timeline of events (now in the calendar), finding her purpose and passion for life. She is starting a candle-making business, and since I started writing this chapter, she dropped off her beautiful candles... which I'll be using going forward as part of the creation on the 'spa' experience. (www.lunarlove.ca - WOW). I can't wait to watch Nicole's journey as she taps into her frequency and designs the life she loves.

I know after every session, and every compliment/testimonial or referral, that I've found my true success by being an influential businesswoman making a difference in people's lives.

Then a Pandemic Hits

Since I wrote this chapter and now that the Covid Pandemic is taking place, I've been thinking "what would I do differently?", or "what is this teaching me?", and here are my thoughts.

I think the forced slowdown will help me with what I'm trying to teach people about being in control to design their lives. A big part of enjoying life more is to slow down, or focus on the things that bring joy, happiness and contentment. Being financially free is all about not thinking about money but having enough that you don't think about it, and that money flows in and out as a tool to enjoy your ideal life.

Also, looking at the business with more of an online presence. What a gift... remember the beginning of my story? My childhood self wanted to be a teacher, but I really wanted to be a businesswoman. So I'm now working to take my Design Your Reality business online and creating mini courses so I can teach woman around the world to love their money and life. Of course the "in person" Design Experience will always remain the most precious experience, however, I'll absolutely reach a larger audience and help more woman with their finances, budgets, rental property acquisitions, net-worth management and growth, and continue to expand on the designs around overseas travel and retirement planning by going online.

Finally, I can take this time of isolation to raise my own frequency and continue to design my own beautiful reality. I feel this time is a gift for myself and the world at large

About the Author

Tracy Teskey's mission in life is to elevate the world one financially secure and confident woman at a time. Tracy has been helping people to understand what truly drives them, inside and out. Her ability to design life plans 5 years at a time with ease is her sacred gift. After 25 years in sales & management roles, she decided to help women educate themselves about finances and take control of their life design. Building life designs began as a passion project for friends and family, but soon morphed into the business you see today. Tracy lives in Waterloo and loves to travel the world. She is living her own designed life and you can follow her on social media and pick up some tips and tricks along the way. It is FUN to Design Your Reality!

Connect with Tracy:

www.designyourreality.ca

tracy@designyourreality.ca

https://www.facebook.com/designyourreality.ca/

https://www.instagram.com/designyourreality.ca/

.

CHAPTER ELEVEN

Business is Simple, People are Complicated

By Laurie Hawkins

I grew up on a farm and really, truly hated the farm. I felt like I was called to be in the big city, amongst the lights, the activity, the people. My dream was New York City, being on Wall Street, working in the biggest hotel. If you knew me now, that would make your jaw drop or you would just laugh right out loud. Today, I am the bare-foot, take me to the country for energy, get me far away from the noise and the lights...let me see the stars and the water person. It's funny how you find yourself throughout life in situations that you just can't wait to get out of and then, you realize that you were right where you were meant to be all along.

One of the most pivotal moments in my life happened in my first year of university. My parents made a decision to sell the family farm. This is where I had lived for most of my life, where all of our family memories were. The place that I couldn't wait to escape would now be gone forever. It was a surreal experience. I realized how much I had learned and grown from the seat of a tractor. I understood what the farm really meant and through the years, I have come to a place of deep gratitude for my roots. The farm shaped me, the country built me, the community created me...I will forever be a farm girl and I'm so very proud of it.

More than that, though, I had a deep awareness that in the middle of what pushes your buttons, stretches your comfort, makes you freak out and feel vulnerable – those are the places where you grow the most, where you realize who you are, where you take the most profound steps towards becoming you! It's the stones that seemed too big to lift, and the boss whose values rubbed deeply against mine, and the marriage that brought me to my knees, and the corporate buyout that rattled my leadership beliefs, and the entrepreneur rollercoaster that found me curled up in a ball when it seemed too hard. It's in those deepest, darkest moments that the real you begins to emerge. It's the day after when you stood a little taller, found a little more of your own voice, connected a little more powerfully to your own core values and started to unravel your own love, leadership and loyalty.

Then, just when you think you know who you are, when you believe you are on the path you are meant to travel, when life seems so calm...there will be another storm. Uncertainty shapes the human spirit. As this book began to unfold, a world pandemic, COVID-19, struck and impacted every human in a unique and personal way. We will look back at 2020 as a year of great change and, I hope, great possibility. I don't say that to minimize the pain and suffering that people are experiencing. It's time for humanity to pause, for businesses to question their cores, for people to challenge what's possible. From this place, I want to share a few of the greatest insights that I have experienced through my own career, business and life.

People Want Answers – Give Them Questions

My dad was a business leader whose career took him away from home most weeks. My mom kept the household running (and the farms, which certainly she wouldn't have chosen...that's another story). I have profound memories of wanting answers from my dad when he would return home. We were quite a combination, when I consider we both liked to operate from the question versus the answer. I would hear stories from my friends of the great lectures they received from their parents. When my Dad had a point to make, it was one question! Remarkable the impact that had. I've gone on to study questions and learn the profound connection to our brains when we operate in curiosity. It forces us to leverage our hearts and our minds in order to answer. This is where true wisdom and connection live. What keeps people stuck in the telling? What about the business world has built this belief that the person with the answers is the true expert? What would be possible if instead, we seek the profound questions? What if we explore, strategize, and plan from the place of questions first? How much more creative would we be? How much more could we achieve?

The next time someone wants the answers, pause and wonder how to form the answer into a question and watch their own knowledge grow and expand. When it comes to questions, the most important questions to reveal are those that take you inside yourself. Here are a few of my favourites.

→ Who are you?

It's so natural for us to develop who we are based upon our stories and experiences, what other people have told us, and what the media shares as success. Have you ever explored what you really think and feel? My favourite follow-up to this, as we get stuck in our own minds, is to go deeper by asking, who are you really? Now your heart will wake up and come to truly answer this question.

→ What is your guiding light?

What are the values you desire to operate from and the things that energize your actions? What is your mission and what is the mark you would like to leave on the world? Knowing this will allow you to feel purpose in your life's work. As a follow-up to this, what is truly unmoveable for you?

→ Where are you going?

Stephen Covey would have called this your 'end in mind'. It's the place you desire to arrive at on your journey. Although you may course-correct along the way, knowing where you are going allows you to take one step forward. It's always about that one next step towards that place.

→ Where did you come from?

Yes, I start with where you are going on purpose. When we look forward, then we can reflect on the times to the now and understand the gap. This becomes the roadmap or success path to adventure, moment by moment. A wonderful next question is, how do you keep going or where do you course-correct as required?

→ Why me?

This is a powerful question when aligned with the right intention. This is not to be asked from a place of judgement. This is to come from a pure place of curiosity. What makes you unique? What attracts people to want to do business with you? What makes you stand out in a sea of the same? What makes you powerfully and authentically you?

→ What else is possible?

This is the power question, the one that unleashes your creativity and positivity, even when asked in tough times. This is the 'snap out of autopilot' cue. Imagine that you are in the thick of something and you pause to ask yourself this power question! Stop yourself in your tracks and turn around your thinking, your feelings, your attitude, your experience. Have fun with this one.

It may be surprising to hear me say that this is one of the most underutilized skills in the human experience. I've been in sales and leadership for over 3 decades and still find very few people that practice the art of curiosity. What can you do from this day forward to embrace this powerful art? How can you sit in curiosity in your life and business?

People Put Books on a Shelf – Bring Them to Life

You take a training course – they give you a big binder of your learnings – you put them on a shelf, never to be touched again. Someone tells you about the latest book that you just have to read – you go to Amazon and click 'buy' – you put it on your shelf until finally you donate it, as you realize that it just isn't going to happen. When I began my business, one of the first things I remember saying was that I didn't want to be another "binder on a shelf" training program. I wanted to impact and influence people and organizations to experience long-term, sustainable growth and change. I desire the same for my bookshelf; that it is a living, breathing thing. Some books I read, take the golden nugget from, and pay them forward to someone else. Others are here for a lifetime, to pull from the shelf for that one insight that is needed in the moment. I've shared my top 30 lifetime books and one quote for each at the end of this book. I hope you enjoy and watch them dance off the page.

Leaders are learners. I believe that at the core depths of my soul. You are either learning or you are falling back. There is no standing still in today's complex environment. Learning doesn't have to be in the form of reading a book. There are so many ways to learn today – perhaps it's a podcast, a YouTube video, a guided meditation. You find your way and lean into expanding your horizons.

People are Complicated – Business is Simple

I worked for a small, innovative telecommunications company back when competition in this industry was beginning to flourish. Canada had, for the most part, been a monopoly. As this started to shift, the industry went through massive disruption. Those days were fast-paced, exciting and creative. It was all about the sale! As I moved into leadership, I gained a new perspective. There was no formal leadership development and what I had learned about being a leader up until that point came more from growing up on a farm, seeing my Dad in action, and sadly, what I could call the negativity of corporate leadership. I was still in that industry as the curve shifted back the other way and now, we are back to the older model again. Our company was purchased by one of the big guys and I spent two years learning everything about what I wouldn't want to be-do-have as a leader. I had a deep yearning to make a difference for people. We did things differently on our team, and took a struggling team to the top team in the country. How did that happen? What did we do differently? I asked myself so many questions and yet, it would still take me a couple of decades in business to reflect back and have the true aha moments.

What I learned was that business itself really isn't that complicated. It is complex and layered and requires strategy and planning. The complicated part of business is the people. You need the people for a business to flourish. This is why the leadership of people is the most critical imperative in any organization, including for entrepreneurs. Looking back, the one thing I realized is that I loved my people...I mean really loved them. I cared about their success, their growth, their families, their dreams. It was personal to me...we were family. In a sales environment we built a team who would fight as hard for the team's success as their individual success. We had a mission that we all lived for. I found out later that when they put me in the leadership role, they intended to close our office. I had been in the top 3 sales performers in the country for a few years and gained the Leaders Circle top rep one year. They didn't want to put me into the role as that would take away the results from our office. They also didn't see our team surviving, and so it was a temporary fix. I didn't know this, though, and so we started at ground zero and although I called us the Bad News Bears, as it did appear that we had no chance of changing the story...we changed the story. With love; for each other, for our customers and for our results.

People are Interested – Teach Them Commitment

Are you committed or just interested? What is the difference? Have you ever set out to achieve a goal and then somewhere along the way lost the energy required to achieve that goal? This is one of the hardest lessons to explore in life. You set that New Year's resolution and then by February 1st, if even that long, you have already thrown in the towel on your resolution.

When I first started my career in telecommunication sales, I had these big dreams. I was going to do amazingly and then move into management as soon as possible. Our VP came to our office after I had been with the company for about three months. I had so much to learn...a new industry, a new style of selling, new customers, a new team. It was all so new. I had worked for the two years prior as the first female sales rep in the wood products industry in Canada. This role had been all about building relationships, sustaining existing customers and learning about their businesses. At the time, telecom was "cut-throat" and very price focused. Still, when our VP came to visit, I felt that I should take the opportunity to share with her my desire to get into management in the future. The tables turned quickly as she informed me that if my sales didn't improve, I would be fired, and I should focus on that instead. Only three months in and this is where I sat. Something inside me changed that day. I became fully committed to my results...not just interested. When you are committed, you do the hard work, you make the extra phone call, you sit in uncomfortableness, you develop the new skill, you become more curious, you dig deep - you make it happen.

Now when I look at a new adventure, new opportunity, a new possibility, I always ask myself – am I committed or just interested? It's ok to have things that I am just interested in, as long as I am honest with myself. I've come to understand that the difference between achieving your mission in life and business is all directly correlated to your commitment.

People Want Logic – Lead with Love

There is logic and there is emotion. There is right brain and there is left brain. We are all so different in our personalities, behaviours, problem-solving, and perspectives. My husband and I are complete opposites on all of these fronts. No matter what assessments we do, we are on polar opposite spectrums. The whole conversation of logic versus emotion has been at the epicentre of many of our conversations through the years. He begins with logic and then eventually lands at attaching emotion. I, on the other hand, begin with emotion and then pull logic into the situation. Either way, we both explore and intertwine all aspects. This is true of all people. Even when someone tells you they make a decision fully based on logic, their emotion is in the driver's seat. Someone shares that they bought a new car because of the colour and price and the specific attributes of the car, and yet it's really about how they feel when they drive it (they just don't realize it).

Recently I asked my son who his favourite hockey coach had been throughout his years of playing sports. He shared with me that it was his first coach, Rob Welch, who coached him with the London Junior Knights. I asked him to explain what it was about Rob that made him his favourite and he said two things: he cared more about the kids than the game (and he cared deeply about the game) and he made it fun. The year we played with Rob, they were on the ice 6 days a week and yet he still remembers the fun moments. They worked hard that year. Rob had high expectations of the kids and their success. I will never forget the moment we had the first parent meeting and Rob told us that it was as important to him to develop young men with impeccable values as it was for him to win hockey games. He did that and to this day, had a powerful impact on not just my son, but all of his players. They also won everything that year. Interesting!

When you lead with love, compassion, connection and build a sense of belonging, that's when a level of achievement truly unfolds in ways that you can't even imagine.

People Say Yes when they Mean No – Learn the Hell Yes

I left the corporate world at the end of 2007 and went on a quest to create a dynamic consulting business. I had this deep calling to ignite people, evolve business and inspire change in the business world. I knew absolutely nothing about starting my own business. I met with over 20 business owners in this market and asked them so many questions about their experiences and insights. I met some incredible people and was in awe of what they had created. I am so grateful for the time they invested with me. It impacted me and I hope that I impart that same type of wisdom to those that are seeking mentorship as they begin on their own journeys.

I launched Hawk Inspired early in 2009 with so much energy, passion, enthusiasm and of course, a plan to change the world. My calendar was filled with networking events, I joined several entrepreneurial groups for connections, and I went to every event in the surrounding area where there were other business people. I said yes to everything. About six months into my business, I had what I now refer to as a full-on entrepreneurial meltdown. It felt like the walls were caving in around me and I just fell to the ground in the middle of our living room and cried my eyes out. I had thrived in my corporate career, achieved incredible levels of success and now, I didn't know what I was doing. I was busier than I could ever have imagined and yet I'd had no real results. I couldn't "sell" myself. My confidence was rock bottom. How could I have done this to my family? What had I done?

It was time to peel back the onion, to do for myself what came so naturally to do for others. Layer by layer, I uncovered some real truths about myself. One of the key things was this need to please others, this constant saying yes to everything, to everyone, and then being overwhelmed, disappointed, frustrated...and going so off-course from the strategy of the business. In my heart, I could feel the no, in my brain, I could hear the no, and then out of my mouth would come the yes. I started to resent the yes. I started to lose focus and even when it was a real yes, I didn't have the energy or time to make it amazing. Something had to change. Then I did something drastic because I had no idea where to begin. I stopped it all...yes, everything. I quit all the groups, I stopped going to events, I stopped booking coffee meetings, I stopped it all. For 6 months, I stayed the course on building business. Everything went through the filter of the business vision, mission and strategy. Revenue generating focus. Period.

This decision was the golden ticket to building a real business. I leaned into this strategy for the next two years and Hawk Inspired flourished. I was still missing something, though. I had become so regimented on the "no" that a piece of my soul was shut off. Time to explore again...and it was at this time that I came up with a new strategy. This was the "hell yes" litmus test. I had to feel and think on a deep level a "hell yes" when choosing to engage in anything moving forward. I incorporated this for life and business. With customer opportunities, with connection opportunities...with anything, really. Then I knew that I would be deeply engaged with my mind, body and spirit. It has been a critical choice for my health, wellbeing and success.

People Want to be Heard – Lose the Cape

I mentioned already that my husband and myself are two very different people. He is superman...well, he thinks he is, and so we all try hard to appease him and allow him to live in his superhero world. You see, he always has the answer, the opinion and the cape on. He wants to solve the problem, rescue the distressed person, answer the call...always. Not sometimes, always. His heart is huge. His desire to help others is unprecedented. He is amazing.

I'm a problem solver too...an inherent helper and coach. We differ in that I ask the questions to get you there and he likes to give the answers. There is no right or wrong in either; it's just how we are hard-wired internally. It's in our DNA. Sometimes, I desire an answer and most of the time I just want to be heard. I love his perspectives and it's of huge value to me that he does think so differently. I have the opportunity to see things from a whole different lens. That is an invaluable gift to me. AND...it's so frustrating when someone goes into the mode of telling you how to fix something when you just what to share and vent a little bit.

It took us a decade together to navigate through this. There might have been some tense moments through that decade – you know exactly what I am talking about! We have the benefit of studying leadership, human psychology, knowing each other's profiles through assessments, deepening our communication awareness to guide teams and leaders and yet we still struggled to get it right together. Funny how that works! Then one day, I asked him to take off the cape and just listen. That was the key. Just ask ahead. Now I preface these situations with what I need in the moment and he truly is a superhero, adapting easily to my needs. I think he probably still has the vision of himself wearing the cape but at least it isn't visible to me in those moments. People really want to know that their voice is heard. How can you remove the cape and lean into what they need?

People Look in the Rear-View Mirror & Crystal Ball – Lean into Presence

Which one do you focus on? Our nature is to be either past- or future-focused. If you are more of a past-focused person, you look in the rear-view of what your life and experiences have been. If you are more of a future person, you are dreaming and planning for what is to come. Being present is the place to be. Being...not doing, not planning...being. My dear friend, Harold Byne, spoke to me one day about how there is nowhere in the bible that talks about human doings; it talks about human beings. That thought changed my whole perspective on how I was living my life.

I'm the dreamer – the visionary – the move forward – the 'what's next?' person. Part of this is who I am and part of this is from my experiences. Growing up, our household was very achievement-focused. What's the goal, what's the next target, how will you improve, what will you do next? Then I moved into a career in sales, which is all about that next achievement. You made quota last month...doesn't matter, go get the next sale. Always moving forward. It's rare for me to look back. Becoming a mom and a business owner started to shift my perspective on always looking for the next mountain to climb. It felt like a gnawing in my stomach. I knew there needed to be a pause but I didn't know what that looked like, felt like, how to do it, or where to begin. If I stopped always doing, could I still succeed in the way I had created? My big moment of awakening came when we were bought by one of the big telecom giants and I saw the behaviours of people. I had little kids at that time and I started noticing this pull between being a present mom and always being on for work. There was an expectation that work came first with this corporation. If you wanted to succeed in leadership in this company, you would have to sell a bit of your family soul. When I left there, I remember coming home, putting my cell phone in a basket and leaving it there for a month. I worked for a mobile phone company...the phone was always on and that was in the early part of

2000! It's been 2 decades of a journey to learn to pause, to focus on being present, to embrace the moments. I am a better mom, wife, friend and absolutely a better business owner for learning how to live in the now. I will say that it frustrates people when they can't reach me and I am sorry for that...I'm being present with someone else in those moments, the same as I choose to be present with you when we are together.

People are on Autopilot – Break Them Out

Have you ever driven home from work and not remembered if you even stopped at the stop signs? You pull in your driveway and can't remember anything about the drive. You are so used to doing the same thing all the time that you do it automatically. I went to a marketing training session a couple of years ago and they had us do an exercise where we looked up other people that were in the same market/business as us. What we found was unbelievable; each site used the same words, same colours, same photos. We were all sounding, looking, feeling the same. It was like a sea of the same. This is autopilot. Seth Godin speaks in his Book called _Purple Cow: Transform Your Business by Being Remarkable_ about the concept of standing out in a sea of the same. After reading this book and going through this exercise, I took a hard look at my own business. In sales I was always taught that it was you who made things different. How can you do that if you are operating on autopilot all the time?

COVID-19 has really snapped people out of autopilot. It's turned routines upside down. The last time I went out to my car and drove somewhere, it felt awkward. It has forced businesses to look at their systems, their communication, their leadership...everything! As I reflected on this for myself, I realized the importance of building a process into my own business to snap out of autopilot every month, every year. I use an exercise now called stop-start-more-less at the end of every 30 days. I ask what to stop doing, what to start doing, what to do more of and what to do less of. This has served as a powerful way to break the brain out of autopilot. I think it's time we all take the wheel and be more purposeful.

People Have Their Own Perspectives – Move Past Judgement

I'm rewriting this section after the past week. Not only have we been months in a pandemic that is rocking our world, at this very moment there are riots happening around the United States and World, in reaction to another horrific killing that took place at the hands of a police officer. I don't want to use this book to discuss the depths of this challenge, but I do want to leverage this as a highlight on the topic of judgement. Our world is riddled with judgement. This judgement drives dissention, hate, fear. We have two choices – love or fear. They don't coexist.

I was a couple of years into my business and one night after we had been out with friends, my husband said to me, "I've noticed that you have become quite judgemental of people lately". Well you can imagine how I felt about hearing those words. That wasn't how I was raised, it wasn't the value I put on myself and yet, as I took a long, hard look in the mirror, I saw he was right. Now I had to peel back that onion again. It wasn't about anyone else. It was about me and some of my own insecurities. I had to do the work to understand my own self-doubt and then I could show up the way that I really wanted - with love towards all others.

We are one human race. The current challenges are a question for humanity. They are an opportunity for humanity. Love really is the answer. Leading with love, leaning in with compassion, focusing on humanity, encouraging others. We need to build connections heart to heart, person to person, human to human. The businesses of tomorrow will deeply understand this truth and build cultures that are rich in compassion, empathy and connection.

People Think Busy is Productive – Teach Effectiveness

Did you realize that people changed the way business was spelt? Somewhere along the way it was adjusted to busyness. I have been so guilty of this in my past. We measure by the whites of people's eyes, the number of hours they put in, how many things they have on their to-do list, how many yes's they say (not hell yes's)! I'm embarrassed to share that when I received a President's Club award once I had become a leader, the CEO shared a story about me from the stage. He spoke about my work ethic and how he had never worked with anyone that you might get an email from at 1am or 5am and how awesome that was. I wore it like a badge of honour. Then, one day, one of the sales people on my team asked to meet with me. He said that his work was affecting his home life. As I asked him to share the challenges with me, it came down to him believing that he had to be checking his email all the time in order to respond to me when I sent a note...whether that was at 1am or 5am or any other time. I did not have the expectation that he would answer me right away but I learned a valuable leadership lesson that day. As the leader goes...so will their people. If I was living that behaviour, then so would the people on my team. It didn't matter that I talked about family and balance. They watched my behaviour.

What they didn't see were the boundaries and reasons behind my work style. They knew that I left work at 4pm every day so I could eat dinner with my family. They knew they couldn't reach me from 4-8pm ever as that was Mama time. They didn't know that my marriage was very unhealthy and unstable and I found great joy in working at night when the kids were in bed. It gave me such a sense of purpose. I loved my work and so it was my choice. It wasn't sustainable, though, and I eventually burned out. It was then that I realized that it was about effectiveness...how can you be effective and achieve your desired outcomes in less time? That's the question. Back to human beings versus human doings.

We've become obsessed with our devices in our world today. For some reason, people don't realize they have choices. You have a choice. You are more effective when you put boundaries around your availability, and when you design your own life instead of allow others to design it. Take the time to connect with how you are most effective.

People Shouldn't Cry When They Play Baseball – That's True

Tom Hanks made famous the saying, "there's no crying in baseball" in the movie *A League of Their Own*. It makes me think about vulnerability and transparency. When you are willing to be vulnerable, you build trust. I am so connected to people that share their trials, their truths, their emotions, their mistakes.

I actually don't think there should be crying in baseball because it should be fun. No matter what level you play at, you should have a smile on your face. There will be tough games and moments but you play for the joy. The challenge in life and business is when the joy is taken. The more fun, the more joy, the more success. Business should be fun...people should be having fun. That leads me to my #popthecork experience.

People Forget to Pause – Pop the Cork

You may have figured out by now that I am a recovering workaholic. It has taken practice, determination and deep healing for me to learn to pause. I know the signs now when I am "efforting" instead of being in the flow and ease of what is truly possible.

I am very blessed to still have a group of amazing girl-friends from public and high school days. We've moved around, had families, lost touch, regained touch...ebbed and flowed as life does. Then, when we were about to all turn 50, we started talking about how to celebrate that. We have a leader and her name is Tracy. She is our walk-ing angel that through all these years has maintained connection with all of us and therefore maintained a group connection. As we started dreaming about what this could look like, we decided that as there were 13 of us, what if each person took a month and was responsible for creating a celebration in that month? It could be anything from taking a hike, to a cider tour, to a Dominican trip, to a sleepover. We spent one full year celebrating turning 50. The reconnection, the laughs, and the memories were amazing. Celebrating like this was a realization of the pause for me. It took 50 years for me to understand the real importance of celebration and the power when mixed with the connection of others.

In this same year, I decided to do something else. Every month, I would go to a new body of water and pop a bottle of champagne and watch the ease and power of the water. I love the water. It revives me. Before this, I would not have wanted to "waste" time. In this year, I felt the re-energization from taking this time. I was more effective, more present, more connected, more alive.

I look at these as philosophies for business and life. Taking moments to celebrate, to pause, to laugh, to share…these all build a new energy within us. This is the inside work that creates a new outer light that shines for all to see. This attracts people to you in powerful ways.

Then a Pandemic Hits

Does a pandemic have to hit to pause before we reflect on how our businesses need to adapt and adjust? You've heard that change is constant. That is true and yet change has a new face. Its pace is accelerated, changes are smaller and more frequent, and it's mixed with new technology that enables even more frequent change. The truth of this requires businesses to be ready to pivot at any moment. The problem you solved for your customers today might require a very different perspective tomorrow. Being mindful, attentive and informed are keys to the game of business today.

In 2019 I had a voice within me telling me that it was time to pivot. I would talk back to that voice...why? The business is successful, I love my work, my customers are incredible and achieving new results...why change a good thing? The voice would answer back and tell me that it was time to pivot. The world needed something that I had to offer – it was time to become bold and start sharing the importance of love in leadership. The voice got louder. I do say that God whispers and then he just keeps getting louder until you have no choice but to listen up. I had started the journey of this pivot, to put the pieces together, to do my research - and then COVID arrived. We had to listen. Every business, every human...it was time to wake up and listen. The reality is, though, we should be doing that all the time. We should be reflecting on our businesses through the scope of what is possible at all times. I would like to share three key lessons that I learned through this experience that would apply to starting a new business, adapting to new environments, or analyzing the scope of your business at any time. There are so many, so I will hone in on only three at this time.

1) Your Confidence Must Trump Their Uncertainty

Being a leader in your field, in your business, in your home, requires confidence. There will always be uncertainty. It will come dressed differently at different times. It will come when you least expect it. When this happens, your customers, your team, your peers, and your family will experience fear, concern, and confusion, and be looking to you for answers. You may not have the answers. You may be feeling and experiencing the exact same emotions as them.

When the pandemic was announced I had one child on a plane to Switzerland and another studying abroad and living in the UK. I felt fear, confusion, and anxiety towards what to do to protect them. It took a couple of weeks for the UK to shut down and we waited to receive word from the school that my daughter could come home without it affecting her education. She has since finished her Post Graduate Education Certificate online. Within days of arriving, my son was also back on a plane home with his girlfriend. So many emotions. I shared my emotions, and yet remained more confident than my children. The same has been through mergers, downsizing, product changes and any other business challenge.

Your confidence as a leader must trump the uncertainty that those around you are experiencing. This doesn't mean you aren't vulnerable and authentic. It's critical that you are. It's also critical that you create consistent communication that builds confidence. There are so many examples of leaders who instill confidence and those that create confusion and fear. These times have shown us the true power of leaders with influence. Think of examples of both of these and explore what insights you can gain from each of them.

2) Look Within to go Beyond

We live in an externally focused world. We watch social media and YouTube videos for both entertainment and education. We judge ourselves against an external view to someone else's life and/or business. We make decisions based upon these external resources. This became so evident to me as a business owner. I would research other people's websites or materials to compare what I could do better, differently, more effectively. I would take training course after training course, seeking the golden nugget that would take me to that next level. When I was in creation mode I would dive into book after book and video after video to find the knowledge to create. I have a strong faith, and yet I realized only in the last few years that I was going external instead of internal. I wondered at what point I had lost the ability to hear my own voice. Then it hit me...hard...I had never really listened to my own voice. I used to hear it but then would muddle it with all the external noise. The quest began to listen, except I first had to develop a new muscle to hear.

If I were to begin again today as a business owner, I would listen to that tiny voice inside and follow it. I would harness the power of intuition and awareness. I would build those muscles. There is a knowing and being inside. There is a truth inside. There is the uniquely amazing and powerful being that is YOU on the inside. There are your sacred gifts on the inside.

On the outside is a blend of everybody else and their perspectives, biases, and truths. Until you first go inside to connect on a deep level with your own, you can't effectively leverage what the outside brings forward. Once you begin from the inside then blend it with the opportunities that exist externally, this is where the magic lies.

Let me share what had become a huge hit in the forehead for me on this one. I have an online program and, for a few years, I have had an internal nudge telling me to fully shift to online, to prepare an offering that is easy for people to navigate from anywhere, anytime. I knew this from the depths of my being and always put it to the bottom of my priority list. Had I invested the time and energy to fully lean into this nudge, I would be fully prepared for the current landscape of everything being pushed to online. As it sits, I'm pushing to up-level my programs to align with the market needs. I'm chasing instead of being leading edge. It's been a huge reminder for me of the importance of listening to that internal voice.

3) Intertwine Generosity

What is unique about the coronavirus pandemic is that it pushed the world into their homes. It turned living rooms into classrooms and conference rooms. It turned Zoom into a household name. Everything about the way we work and live has been changed. We've seen fear, overwhelm and anxiety reach a peak throughout our homes and businesses. It has also shown us inspiring acts of kindness from people all around the world. Whether it's frontline workers risking their own lives to save others or grocery store employees who are working tirelessly or companies who are sharing their gifts with their communities, generosity has sprouted as the new cool kid on the block.

Someone showing generosity has a spirit to share their time, money, compassion or kindness to people in need. Generosity is more than money and stuff; it's an energy, a life-force, a true spirit that shines and ripples out in unexpected ways. As I'm typing, the song "what the world needs now, is love sweet love" is humming in my brain. It's hard to hum and type but it's also making me smile. Generosity is a superpower for any business.

Let's look at a few examples: businesses that were not considered essential and had the ability to turn their facilities into manufacturing hand sanitizer and masks, organizations that chose to keep all employees working and protecting them financially, free online training programs, locations giving space for makeshift hospitals...the brands and examples are enormous.

The question is, how do you build this into your business from the beginning? How do you give wings to your vision through a spirit of generosity?

Bonus: Hope Can Transform Anything?

Early in my sales career, we took a training course called "Hope is Not a Strategy" and it was quite powerful. What I took away from that was that it was my responsibility to create the success I desired. Back to the faith piece...you can see the mixed messages that are constantly coming at us. Years later, I remember sitting in my mobile office (my car...which I spent a lot of time up and down highways in) and all of a sudden, that little voice that I didn't listen to enough asked "what if hope is a strategy"? That's an interesting perspective.

When this pandemic hit, Oprah & Deepak offered a free meditation series called *Hope in Uncertain Times.* During this series, Oprah shared that "hope can transform anything" and it created a deep connection to the importance of focusing on hope during these times. Then I expanded on that thought and realized that hope really needs to be at the centre of any business. Think of what you could accomplish if you did have hope as a strategy. It would be like supercharging the battery of your business.

Hope allows you to fall down and get back up. Hope gives you permission to lead with love and compassion. Hope creates loyalty. Hope is remarkable. Hope energizes people. Hope creates influence. Hope emboldens you to think, feel and take action on your strategies. Maybe it's hope that is the energy of your strategy?!

Closing

We come to the end of this gathering of the stories of everyday people; the ones who believed when they were three feet from gold, they needed to lean in and keep digging. The ones who had a tiny voice inside of them telling them to keep going. The ones who knew that their struggles could and would turn into triumph if they kept believing and taking action. My hope for you is that you will take at least one insight, idea or inspiration away with you to guide you on your own journey.

About the Author

Laurie Hawkins is a curator, catalyst and connector. She is a certified business success strategist, speaker, radio show host, trainer and leader who drives revenue, results and raving fans along with fulfillment and flow. Laurie's reputation is built on her unique ability to enable strategy and soul to coexist. She is a thought-leader with the rare ability to both inspire and create actionable strategies.

Daily, she inspires people across all of her platforms; Instagram, YouTube, Facebook, Podcast, Blog and Live to create impact and influence. An award-winning leader in business for more than 25 years, Laurie is focused on using her expertise to guide high-level leaders and business owners to become influencers in their industry, business and lifeI am Laurie Hawkins.

In Laurie's Words:

I show up for the driven ambitious leaders, brilliant minds, rebel hearts and up-levellers. Like you, I am on a life-long adventure to inspire, encourage and equip people to become the very best version of themselves, by focusing on reinvention, smashing the status quo and never accepting mediocrity.

I believe...

- I believe in progress over perfection (I say this now as I am a recovering perfectionist)! I'm committed to being as straight up and kind as possible and meaningful for the situation you are in right now!

- I believe in the power of gaining insights and wisdom, which is why I buy every book and educational program possible. Yes, I am a knowledge hoarder. (See my must read insights in this book)

- I believe that gratitude and generosity keep the Universe in collaboration with you and that the greatest gift you can give yourself and those you love is a healthy you.

- I believe that we all have a unique destiny to fulfill in this lifetime. Mine may be buying expensive pens and then hiding them from my husband as he thinks that all pens write the same!?

- I believe that everything should be turned into an experience AND that hope is the fuel of creation. Even though I know this, I binge watch Netflix because I just can't wait for the story to unfold.

- I believe in celebrating grace over guilt, creating belonging over fitting in and leading with love in all things.

- I believe in the power of exploring new things, in bare feet, with a glass of bubbly in your hand because curiosity and fascination open up new possibilities.

Accomplishments

- Leaders Circle Sales Award for Top Sales Nationally at one of Canada's Fortune 50 companies.

- 10 consecutive years of Presidents Club Sales Awards at one of Forbes Global 2000 listed companies.

- Ritz Carlton Service Excellence Leadership Training

- IVEY School of Business Leadership

- Increased revenue, results & raving fans with teams, businesses and corporations that are top in their industries and markets.

- Accelerated the impact and influence of entrepreneurs, business owners and leaders across unique industries.

- Chair of the Board for multiple boards

- Certified Sacred Gifts Facilitator

- Certified DISC, MBTI & other assessment tools to enhance personal communication, amplify team synergy and build organizational culture.

- Human Synergistics Accredited Practitioner

- FocalPoint Certified Business Success Coach

- Gold Duke of Edinburough Award

Connect with Laurie

www.hawkinspired.com

www.facebook.com/StrategySoulLaurie/

www.instagram.com/hawkinspired/

https://www.linkedin.com/in/hawkinspired/

www.youtube.com/user/TheHawkInspired

Books Brought to Life

By Laurie Hawkins

Since I speak of how books have shaped me so profoundly, I wanted to share my foundational readings. These are the books that have been pivotal at very specific points in my life. I shared my beliefs around "binders on a shelf" and so I always giggle a little when I see my shelves so filled with books. No dust though...I actually think they may all share stories, drink some bubbly and dance a little even while I am sleeping. These are the books that will always hold a special spot in my heart and on my shelves and here is a piece of wisdom from each one.

♥ Awakening Corporate Soul – Four Paths to Unleash the Power of People at Work, Eric Klein & John B. Izzo. Publisher: Fairwinds Press, 1998

  → "From the human perspective, the crisis is highly personal and threatens the inner sense of purpose, caring and vitality that makes work meaningful. Millions of workers feel burned out, overworked and stressed to the max with a deep sense of having sacrificed too much of their personal lives for the corporate good. A quest for something more is brewing inside workers from the shop floor to the top of the corporate ladder. It is a crisis of soul that can only be resolved by the awakening of what we call Corporate Soul."

♥ Love Does – Discover a Secretly Incredible Life in an Ordinary World, Bob Goff. Publisher: Nelson Books, 2012

→ "I used to be afraid of failing at the things that really mattered to me, but now I'm more afraid of succeeding at the things that don't matter."

♥ The War of Art – Break Through the Blocks and Win Your Inner Creative Battles, Steven Pressfield. Publisher: Black Irish Entertainment LLC, 2019

→ "Resistance is the most toxic force on the planet. It is the root of more unhappiness than poverty, disease...to yield to resistance deforms our spirit....it prevents us from achieving the life God intended when He endowed each of us with our own unique genius. Genius...is our soul's seat, the vessel that holds our being-in-potential, our star's beacon and Polaris. Every sun casts a shadow, and genius's shadow is resistance. As powerful as our soul's call to realization, so potent are the forces of resistance arrayed against it."

♥ The Four Agreements – The Practical Guide to Personal Freedom, Don Miguel Ruiz. Publisher: Amber Allen Publishing Inc., 2005

→ "You achieve the mastery of transformation by changing the fear-based agreements that make you suffer and reprogramming your own mind, in your own way."

♥ The Traveller's Gift – Seven Decisions that Determine Personal Success, Andy Andrews. Publisher: Thomas Nelson, 2002

→ "Reason can only be stretched so far, but faith has no limits. The only limit to your realization of tomorrow is the doubt you hold fast today."

♥ Present over Perfect – Leaving Behind Frantic for a Simpler, More Soulful Way of Living, Shauna Niequist. Publisher: Zondervan, 2016

→ "The more I listen to myself, my body, my feelings, and the less I listen to the 'should' and 'must' and 'to-do' voices, the more I realize my body and spirit have been whispering all along, but I couldn't hear them over the chaos and noise of the life I'd created. I was addicted to this chaos, but like any addiction, it was damaging to me. Here's what I know: I thought the doing and the busyness would keep me safe. They keep me numb. Which is not the same as safe, which isn't even the greatest thing to aspire to. If you're not like me – prone to frantic levels of activity, swirling chaos, fast-moving cycles of over-commitment and resentment – then you might press your face up to the glass of my life with something like wonder and a little confusion."

♥ A Return to Love – Reflections on the Principles of a Course in Miracles, Marianne Williamson. Publisher: HarperOne, 1996

→ "As we begin to understand more deeply why love is such a necessary element in the healing of the world, a shift will occur in how we live our lives within and without."

♥ The 5 Love Languages – The Secret to Love That Lasts, Gary Chapman. Publisher: Northfield Publishing, 2015

→ "Without love, I may spend a lifetime in search of significance, self-worth and security. When I experience love, it influences all those needs positively. I am now free to develop my potential. I am more secure in my self-worth and can now turn my efforts outward instead of being obsessed with my own needs. Love liberates. Love is a choice."

♥ The Untethered Soul – The Journey Beyond Yourself, Michael A. Singer. Publisher: New Harbinger Publications, 2007

→ "True personal growth is about transcending the part of you that is not okay and needs protection. This is done by constantly remembering that you are the one inside that notices the voice talking. That is the way out. The one inside who is aware that you are always talking to yourself about yourself is always silent. It is a doorway to the depths of your being. To be aware that you are watching the voice talk is to stand on the threshold of a fantastic inner journey. If used properly, the same mental voice that has been a source of worry, distraction, and general neurosis can become the launching ground for true spiritual awakening. Come to know the one who watches the voice and you will come to know one of the great mysteries of creation."

♥ The Seat of the Soul, Gary Zukav. Publisher: Simon & Schuster, 2014

→ "When the personality comes fully to serve the energy of its soul, that is authentic empowerment."

♥ Scary Close – Dropping the Act and Finding True Intimacy, Donald Miller. Publisher: Nelson Books, 2015

→ "When the story of earth is told, all that will be remembered is the truth we exchanged. The vulnerable moments. The terrifying risk of love and the care we took to cultivate it. And all the rest, the distracting noises of insecurity and the flattery and the flashbulbs will flicker out."

- ♥ The Energy Bus – 10 Rules to Fuel Your life, Work and Team with Positive Energy, Jon Gordon. Publisher: Wiley, 2007

  → "The fuel that moves you and your team to your destination is positive energy. Real positive energy comes from trust, faith, enthusiasm, purpose, joy and happiness. The power of positive energy can change lives and the entire world and it starts with each person fueling themselves with positive energy so they can share it with others."

- ♥ Becoming a Category of One – How Extraordinary Companies Transcend Commodity and Defy Comparison, Joe Calloway. Publisher: Wiley, 2009

  → "Category of One companies want their customers to think of them differently, and instill that desire in their employees. These organizations strive to know more about their customers than anyone else. They want to come closer to their customers than any potential rivals could. They wish to connect emotionally with their customers more completely than anyone else. Customer service is an ancient business precept, but surprisingly many organizations fail to build their operations on that simple rule. Category of One companies, in contrast, are dedicated to winning and keeping loyal customers for life."

- ♥ Delivering Happiness – A Path to Profits, Passion and Purpose, Tony Hsieh. Publisher: Grand Central Publishing, 2013

    → "I made a note to myself to make sure I never lost sight of the value of a tribe where people truly felt connected and cared about the well-being of one another. To me, connectedness, the number and depth of my relationships, was an important element of my happiness, and I was grateful for our tribe."

- ♥ Manifesting Change – It Couldn't Be Easier, Mike Dooley. Publisher: Atria Books/Beyond Words, 2011

    → "Everything that's happened and is happening now is playing to your favour. Let this be your modus operandi and remember: throughout every journey, the miracles of progress are almost always invisible. What surrounds you today is no indicator of what's going to unfold tomorrow. Where you are is never who you are."

- ♥ Change Your Questions Change Your Life - 10 Powerful Tools for Life and Work, Marilee Adams. Publisher: Berrett -Koehler Publishers, 2016

    → "Questions are like treasures hidden in broad daylight."

- ♥ The Invitation, Oriah. Publisher: HarperOne, 2006

    → "It doesn't interest me what you do for a living. I want to know what you ache for and if you dare to dream of meeting your heart's longing."

- ♥ The Gifts of Imperfection – Let Go of Who You Think You're Supposed to be and Embrace Who You Are, Brene Brown. Publisher: Hazelden Publishing, 2010

    → "Wholehearted living is about engaging in our lives from a place of worthiness. It means cultivating the courage, compassion and connection to wake up in the morning and think; no matter what gets done and how much is left undone, I am enough. It's going to bed at night thinking; yes, I am imperfect and vulnerable and sometimes afraid, but that doesn't change the truth that I am also brave and worthy of love and belonging."

- ♥ Your One Word – The Powerful Secret to Creating a Business and Life That Matter, Evan Carmichael. Publisher: TarcherPerigree, 2016

    - → "Every decision you make in your life and business will become easier. Door will start to open where before you struggled to make any progress. You'll finally feel like you're living your life with a purpose instead of fighting the world around you."

- ♥ The Five Dysfunctions of a Team – A Leadership Fable, Patrick Lencioni. Publisher: Jossey-Bass, 2002

    - → "Teamwork remains the one sustainable competitive advantage that has been largely untapped."

- ♥ Purple Cow – Transform Your Business by Being Remarkable, Seth Godin. Publisher: Penguin Books, 2007

    - → "The leader is the leader because he did something remarkable and that remarkable thing is now taken, it's no longer remarkable when you do it."

♥ Year of Yes – How to Dance it Out, Stand in the Sun and Be Your Own Person, Shonda Rhimes. Publisher: Simon & Schuster, 2016

→ "Downtime is helping to relight that little spark inside; it's helping my creativity and in the long run helping me tell the stories my work needs me to tell. I give myself permission to view this downtime as essential. It's hard to do. It's hard to feel like I deserve any time to replenish the well when I know everyone else is working hard too."

♥ The Book of Joy – Lasting Happiness in a Changing World, Dalai Lama & Desmond Tutu. Publisher: Viking, 2016

→ "The three factors that seem to have the greatest influence on increasing our happiness are our ability to reframe our situation more positively, our ability to experience gratitude, and our choice to be kind and generous. These were exactly the attitudes and actions that the Dalai Lama and the Archbishop would return to as central pillars of joy."

- ♥ Braving the Wilderness – The Quest for True Belonging and the Courage to Stand Alone, Brene Brown. Publisher: Random House Trade Paperbacks, 2019

  → "True belonging is the spiritual practice of believing in and belonging to yourself so deeply that you can share your most authentic self with the world and find sacredness in both being a part of something and standing alone in the wilderness. True belonging doesn't require you to change who you are; it requires you to be who you are."

- ♥ Boundaries – When to Say Yes, How to Say No, To Take Control of Your Life, Dr. Henry Cloud & Dr. John Townsend. Publisher: Zondervan, 2017

  → "This is the path to real love: communicate your boundaries openly."

- ♥ You Can Heal Your Life, Louise L. Hay. Publisher: Hay House Inc., 1984

  → "You have the power to heal your life, and you need to know that. We think so often that we are helpless, but we're not. We always have the power of our minds...claim and consciously use your power."

♥ The Little Red Book of Selling – 12.5 Principles of Sales Greatness, Jeffrey Gitomer. Publisher: Bard Press, 2004

→ "Climbing the ladder of success? Which way are you headed? Hint: the secret to climbing up is to put your heart into your work."

♥ Raving Fans – A Revolutionary Approach to Customer Service, Ken Blanchard & Sheldon Bowles. Publisher: William Morrow, 1993

→ "Your customers are only satisfied because their expectations are so low and because no one else is doing better. Just having satisfied customers isn't good enough anymore. If you really want a booming business, you have to create raving fans."

♥ The Power of Intention – Learning to Co-create Your World Your Way, Dr. Wayne Dyer. Publisher: Hay House Inc., 2005

→ "The qualities of creativity and genius are within you, awaiting your decision to match up with the power of intention."

- ♥ Yay, You – Moving Out, Moving Up, Moving On, Sandra Boynton. Publisher: Little Simon, 2001

    - → "Whatever you do, now or later, big or small, loud or quiet. Whatever you do, don't worry. Just try it. Whatever you do, whether near or so far, I know you'll be great. You already are."

Manufactured by Amazon.ca
Bolton, ON

15710840R00138